Heaven

A seven-session small group discussion guide
companion to the Heaven DVD

Heaven Small Group Discussion Guide

Copyright © 2008 by Lifetogether Publishing and Lamplighter Media

All rights reserved.

ISBN: 978-1-61539-009-0

Acknowledgements

The Heaven Small Group DVD and *Small Group Discussion Guide* have come together through the efforts of many at Tyndale Publishing, Lifetogether Publishing, and Lamplighter Media for which we express our heartfelt thanks.

Executive Producer	John Nill
Producer and Director	Sue Doc Ross
Curriculum Development	Stephanie French, Teresa Haymaker, and Pam Marotta
Director of Photography	Nick Calabrese
Video Location Producers	Brett Eastman and Juan Feldman
Script Writer	Teresa Haymaker
Sound Engineering	Brian Maier and Oziel Jabin Ibarra
Music & Score	Ben Humphries and Oziel Jabin Ibarra
Video Editors	Lance Tracy and Oziel Jabin Ibarra
Video Graphics	Rodney Bissell and Natalie Ibarra
Project Assistant	DeLisa Ivy

Special guest appearance and thanks to:

Randy Alcorn and his family: wife, Nanci Alcorn; daughter Karina, and sons Matthew and Jack Franklin; daughter Angela, and sons Jake and Ty Stump

Ron Beers, Jon Farrar of Tyndale House Publishers

Invitation Speakers: Raul Ries, Bishop George McKinney, and Egla Febe

All involved give full credit to the Lord for his direction and intervention in the making of this series.

TABLE OF CONTENTS

READ ME FIRST

Thank you for selecting the *Heaven Small Group Video Curriculum*. To best utilize the Heaven materials, we recommend that each group have one *Heaven DVD* and a copy of this *Group Discussion Guide* for each group member.

On the *Heaven DVD* there are 7 video sessions taught by Randy Alcorn, small group leader tips, worship songs, leader notes, and bonus footage. DVDs can be purchased separately or as part of a *Heaven Leader's Pack* or *Group Kit*.

This *Group Discussion Guide* is the official companion for the *Heaven DVD*. After watching a video session, the group goes through the *Group Discussion Guide*. Designed to highlight five purposes for successful small groups: fellowship, discipleship, ministry, evangelism, and worship, this *Group Discussion Guide* includes 7 sessions, FAQs, *Reflection* pages, leader notes, and spiritual assessments to chart and track spiritual growth.

For the optimal experience, included are daily *Reflections* that coincide with Randy Alcorn's *50 Days of Heaven* (a compilation of the best of the book *Heaven*). We recommend each household purchase the *50 Days of Heaven* book.

For group leaders who want to dig deeper, *Heaven* books are also available separately or in deluxe *Group Kits*. It is not absolutely necessary to purchase the *Heaven* book, but for those leaders wishing to use the book, we have cross references to pages in the *Heaven* book in this *Group Discussion Guide*.

A typical group session will include the following:

MEMORY VERSE. For each session we have provided a memory verse that emphasizes an important truth. Memorizing this verse is optional, but we believe that memorizing Scripture can be a vital part of renewing and transforming our minds according to the will of God. We encourage you to give this important habit a try.

 CONNECTING WITH GOD'S FAMILY. The foundation for spiritual growth is an intimate connection with God and his family. A few people who really know you and who earn your trust provide a place to experience the life Jesus invites you to live. This section of each session typically offers you an opportunity to get to know your whole group using an icebreaker question.

DVD TEACHING SEGMENT. A DVD companion to this discussion guide is available separately or as part of a *Heaven Leader's Pack* or *Group Kit*. For each study session, the DVD contains a message by Randy Alcorn. View the teaching segment after your *Connecting* time and before the *Growing* section.

GROWING TO BE LIKE CHRIST. Here is where you'll further explore the teaching through discussion. We want to help you understand and apply the Scriptures practically and creatively, allowing God to transform your life from the inside out through the application of God's timeless truths.

DEVELOPING AND SHARING SECTIONS. Each session will include one of the following sections:

DEVELOPING YOUR GIFTS TO SERVE OTHERS. God has designed each of us uniquely to serve him in a way no other person can. Some group sessions will focus on helping you discover and use your God-given abilities.

SHARING YOUR LIFE MISSION EVERY DAY. Jesus wants all of his disciples to help outsiders connect with him, to know him personally. Some group sessions will encourage you to go beyond Bible study to biblical living.

PRAYER AND SURRENDER. God is most pleased by a heart that is fully his. Some group sessions will give you a chance to surrender your heart to God in worship. You may read a Psalm, share the Lord's Supper, or sing a song together to close your meeting. This time will knit your hearts in community and help you surrender your hurts and dreams into the hands of the One who knows you best.

SCRIPTURE STUDY. If you want to dig deeper into the Bible passages about the subject at hand, we've provided suggested study passages in this section. The *Growing* section will provide you with plenty to discuss within the group, so we recommend that participants study these passages on their own between group meetings, if desired.

REFLECTIONS. We encourage you to read seven *Reflections*, one each day, between small group meetings. The suggested *Reflections* and space for journaling each week are listed at the end of each session. If you don't have time to work through all the *Reflections* between group meetings, we suggest you work through the day(s) marked with an asterisk.

INTRODUCTION

We want to welcome you to this exciting study on Heaven. Our prayer for you is to experience the reality of God in a way that really begins to transform your everyday life. God created each of us for a life that is far better than we ever imagined possible, and we want to do all that we can to embrace what he has for us.

As you join us on this journey, we hope you will personally encounter God in a profound way. And as you learn and grow, we hope you will share with others what you are learning. We are very excited that you have decided to join us in this study of Heaven.

In the video for this study on Heaven, Randy Alcorn discusses a renewed perspective of Heaven based on the reality of the present Heaven, the restoration promised in a New Earth, and the rewards of reigning and ruling with God on the New Earth, Eden reclaimed.

There are three phases: life on earth as we now know it, an Intermediate Heaven—the place we go when we die, and the New Heaven and New Earth we will inhabit after the resurrection. These three phases are depicted in the timeline below.

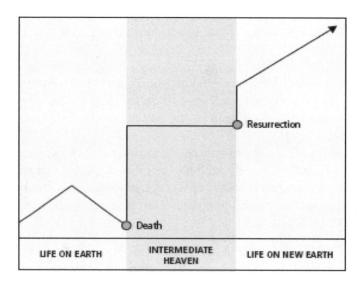

SESSION 1: WHAT WE KNOW ABOUT HEAVEN

Memory Verse: *And I saw the holy city, the new Jerusalem, coming down from God out of heaven like a bride beautifully dressed for her husband. [3] I heard a loud shout from the throne, saying, "Look, God's home is now among his people! He will live with them, and they will be his people. God himself will be with them."* Revelation 21:2–3 (NLT)

Many people don't look forward to Heaven because it is a realm that we lack the ability to see or easily understand. We are naturally hesitant or even fearful in uncertain situations. This session will give us perspective on what Heaven is like.

We have included *Reflections* at the end of each session that correlate to Randy Alcorn's *50 Days of Heaven* book. We suggest you read the *Introduction* and *Days 1* through *7* in the book as you work through the *Reflections*, one each day, before each group meeting. We have provided space at the end of each *Reflection* where you can write your thoughts. These pages are for personal reflection that will not be shared during group time.

If you don't have time to work through all the *Reflections* before the next group meeting, we suggest you work through the day(s) marked with an asterisk.

Open your group with prayer.

Group Values

Attendance. Give priority to the group meeting. Call or email if you will be late or absent.

Environment. Help create a safe place where people can be heard and feel loved. (No quick answers, snap judgments, or simple fixes.)

Respect. Be gentle and gracious—people have different spiritual maturity, personal opinions, and temperaments. Remember, we are all works in progress.

Confidentiality. Keep everything that is shared in the group strictly confidential—no exceptions.

Welcome Newcomers. Keep an open chair and share Jesus' dream of finding a shepherd for every sheep.

Group Ownership. Remember that every member is a minister. Each group member should take on a small role or responsibility in the group over time.

CONNECTING WITH GOD'S FAMILY (10 MIN)

1. Read through the Group Values panel on page 7 (group values are condensed from the *Small Group Agreement* available on groupspice.com). Take some time to reflect on these values together. Choose one or two values to emphasize during this study—values that will take your group to the next stage of intimacy and spiritual health.

2. What do you think Heaven is like?

3. How do you think Heaven compares to our lives here on earth?

4. Who do you think will be in Heaven?

Watch the DVD teaching for this session now. After watching the video, have someone read the discussion questions in the *Growing* section and direct the group discussion.

GROWING TO BE LIKE CHRIST (30 MIN)

Randy Alcorn's books, *Heaven* and *50 Days of Heaven*, were born out of his realization that many people don't really know what Heaven is like. Randy desires to give us purpose, perspective, and hope as we look forward to eternity in a real, tangible Heaven.

5. Based on the video teaching, how has your perspective of Heaven changed?

   Identify and discuss some of the misconceptions people have about Heaven. (*Heaven*, pp. 5–13)

6. In Isaiah 65:17a God says *Behold, I will create new heavens and a new earth* (NIV).

   How does this verse help you see Heaven as a real place? What do you think the New Earth will look like? What will we look like? (*Heaven*, pp. 51-63)

7. One of the criminals crucified with Jesus said to him, *"Jesus, remember me when you come into your kingdom."* [43]*Jesus answered him, "I tell you the truth, today you will be with me in Paradise."* Luke 23:42b–43 (NIV)

   Where is Jesus now according to this verse? What does this say about where believers currently go when they die?

8. One of the biggest misconceptions is that the current Heaven, or Paradise, is our final destination when we die.

   Read Revelation 21:2–3 and discuss where God will ultimately dwell with humankind. (*Heaven*, pp. 41–42)

   We tend to picture the permanent Heaven rather than the temporary one. How does the dwelling place described in Revelation 21:2–3 differ from most people's understanding of Heaven?

9. A New Jerusalem, on the New Earth, will be the dwelling place of all God's children after the Resurrection (see the timeline in the *Introduction*.) Take turns reading Isaiah 65:17–25.

   According to this passage, what kind of place will the New Earth be? How important is this to you? Why? (*Heaven*, pp. 95–99)

10. *For since the creation of the world God's invisible qualities—his eternal power and divine nature—have been clearly seen, being understood from what has been made, so that men are without excuse.* Romans 1:20 (NIV)

   Romans 1:20 speaks of how we can see God today. According to this Scripture, how is God revealed to us? How does God reveal himself to you?

11. Speaking of the New Jerusalem, John said in Revelation 21:26–27, *And all the nations will bring their glory and honor into the city. *²⁷*Nothing evil will be allowed to enter, nor anyone who practices shameful idolatry and dishonesty—but only those whose names are written in the Lamb's Book of Life* (NLT).

    Enter through the narrow gate. For wide is the gate and broad is the road that leads to destruction, and many enter through it. ¹⁴*But small is the gate and narrow the road that leads to life, and only a few find it.* Matthew 7:13–14 (NIV)

    After hearing Randy's teaching today, and reading the verses above, what is the default destination for unbelievers when they die? (*Heaven*, pp. 23–29)

12. Job said *I know that my Redeemer lives, and that in the end he will stand upon the earth.* ²⁶*And after my skin has been destroyed, yet in my flesh I will see God...* Job 19:25–26 (NIV)

    How does this verse give you assurance that you can live for eternity with the Lord?

SHARING YOUR LIFE MISSION EVERY DAY (15 MIN)

We can live with optimism and hope in the midst of all the sin in the world because of Jesus' redemptive work on the cross.

13. Jesus took our sin upon himself, paying the price on our behalf, so that we can be with him for all eternity.

    Since the default destination of unbelievers is hell, what should be our mission?

14. The Bible says, *Since, then, you have been raised with Christ, set your hearts on things above, where Christ is seated at the right hand of God. ²Set your minds on things above, not on earthly things. ³For you died, and your life is now hidden with Christ in God.* Colossians 3:1–3 (NIV)

    God says *Set your minds on things above....* How do you think living your life with an eternal perspective would affect the way you live your life each day?

15. Take a look at the *Circles of Life* diagram below and write in each circle the names of two or three people you know who need to connect in a Christian community like your small group. Commit to praying for God's guidance and an opportunity to invite them to your next group meeting.

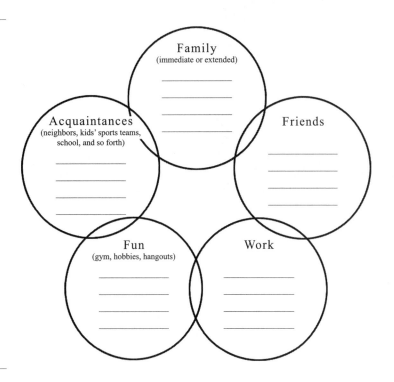

PRAYER AND SURRENDER (10 MIN)

16. This study has revealed many ideas about what Heaven is and is not. You may be surprised about or even disagree with what you've heard. Take a few minutes to pray for your response to this study. Also, ask God to help you find answers to any questions you still have regarding what Heaven is really like.

17. Share prayer requests in your group and record the requests and praises on the *Prayer and Praise Report* beginning on page 123. Commit to praying for each other throughout the week between group meetings.

Note: The contents of the *Reflections* at the end of the session correlate to Randy Alcorn's *50 Days of Heaven* book. We suggest you read the *Introduction* and *Days 1* through *7* in the book as you work through the *Reflections*, one each day, before your next group meeting. We have provided space at the end of each *Reflection* where you can write your thoughts. These pages are for personal reflection that will not be shared during group time. If you don't have time to work through all the *Reflections* before your next group meeting, we suggest you work through the day(s) marked with an asterisk.

SCRIPTURE STUDY

If you want to dig deeper into the Bible passages about the topic at hand, we've provided suggested study passages below. The *Growing* section provides you with plenty to discuss within the group, so we recommend that participants study these passages on their own between group meetings, if desired.

- Colossians 3:1–3
- 1 Corinthians 15:55
- 2 Corinthians 5:6–8
- Ephesians 1:10; 2:8–9
- Exodus 33:18–23
- Galatians 3:13–14
- Genesis 3:8
- Habakkuk 1:13
- Hebrews 2:14–15; 11:16; 12:14; 13:8
- Isaiah 59:2; 65:17–25
- Job 19:25–27
- 1 John 1:9
- John 1:14, 10:30; 14:2, 9, 23; 16:33
- Luke 2:36–38; 10:20; 15:8; 16:19–31; 19:10
- Matthew 1:23, 5:8; 7:12–14; 8:12; 13:45, 18:12; 25:46
- 1 Peter 1:18–19; 3:18
- 2 Peter 3:13
- Philippians 1:21–23; 3:12–14
- Proverbs 28:13
- Psalm 19:1; 27:4; 42:1–2; 63:1; 73:25
- Revelation 21–22
- Romans 1:20; 3:23; 8:20–25, 32
- Romans 12:2
- 1 Timothy 6:16–17
- Titus 3:5

REFLECTIONS

Each day, read a *Reflection* below, giving prayerful consideration to what you learn about God, his Spirit, and his place in your life. If you don't have time to work through all the *Reflections* before your next group meeting, we suggest you work through the day(s) marked with an asterisk.

*Day 1 – If We Can Just See the Shore

If we can learn to fix our eyes on Jesus, to see through the fog of our present trials and circumstances, and picture our eternal home in our mind's eye, it will comfort and energize us, giving us a clear view of the shore—our eternal destination. Like the apostle Paul, we are encouraged to forget what is behind and press on toward the goal to win the prize.

Use the space included for each day to write down any thoughts or feelings that God is putting on your heart.

> *No, dear brothers and sisters, I am still not all I should be, but I am focusing all my energies on this one thing: Forgetting the past and looking forward to what lies ahead, ¹⁴I strain to reach the end of the race and receive the prize for which God, through Christ Jesus, is calling us up to heaven.* Philippians 3:13–14 (NLT)

Reflection: Are you able to see the shore? What is God revealing to you?

_____

_____

_____

_____

_____

_____

Day 2 – Heavenly Minded and of Earthly Good

God commands us to set our hearts and minds on Heaven where Jesus Christ is seated in honor and power. It is an ongoing process. But if we let the truth fuel our imagination and our thoughts, we can be more heavenly minded and of more earthly good.

Since you have been raised to new life with Christ, set your sights on the realities of heaven, where Christ sits at God's right hand in the place of honor and power. [2]Let heaven fill your thoughts. Do not think only about things down here on earth. Colossians 3:1–2 (NLT)

Reflection: As you focus your mind on Heaven and let your imagination soar, what is God revealing to you?

_____

_____

_____

_____

_____

_____

_____

_____

_____

_____

_____

_____

Day 3 – Seeing God's Face

David was preoccupied with God's person and with God's place. He longed to be where God was and to gaze on his beauty. To see God will be our greatest joy.

> *The one thing I ask of the Lord—the thing I seek most—is to live in the house of the Lord all the days of my life, delighting in the Lord's perfections and meditating in his Temple.* Psalm 27:4 (NLT)

Reflection: What do you think it will be like to see God face to face?

_____

_____

_____

_____

_____

_____

_____

_____

_____

_____

_____

_____

_____

_____

Day 4 – Our Primary Pleasure

Job was confident that, in his own flesh, he would see God (Job 19:25–27), and, although Job was a troubled soul, he lived with great anticipation of the day he would see God face to face. We can catch glimpses of God in what he has made (Romans 1:20), and as the provider of everything, he is the source of every pleasure.

> *As the deer longs for streams of water, so I long for you, O God. ²I thirst for God, the living God. When can I go and stand before him?* Psalm 42:1–2 (NLT)

Reflection: How can we learn to see God as the source of every good thing? Think about how this affects your idea of what is important in your life.

_____

_____

_____

_____

_____

_____

_____

_____

_____

_____

_____

_____

_____

Day 5 – Enjoying God in Secondary Pleasures

God richly provides us with everything for our enjoyment (1 Timothy 6:17) and this will not change when we go to Heaven. But these pleasures should never eclipse our love for God, but rather encourage us to give glory to the One who provides.

> *Command those who are rich in this present world not to be arrogant nor to put their hope in wealth, which is so uncertain, but to put their hope in God, who richly provides us with everything for our enjoyment.* 1 Timothy 6:17 (NIV)

Reflection: How can our lives reflect glory to God as we enjoy what he has given us?

_____

_____

_____

_____

_____

_____

_____

_____

_____

_____

_____

_____

_____

Day 6 – Knowing for Sure That We're Going to Heaven

We should not overlook the fact that our sin is sufficient to keep us out of Heaven. Heaven is not our default destination when we die. Jesus Christ offers everyone the gifts of forgiveness, salvation, and eternal life in Heaven.

> *For everyone has sinned; we all fall short of God's glorious standard.* Romans 3:23 (NLT)
>
> *You can enter God's Kingdom only through the narrow gate. The highway to hell is broad, and its gate is wide for the many who choose that way.* [14]*But the gateway to life is very narrow and the road is difficult, and only a few ever find it.* Matthew 7:13–14 (NLT)

Reflection: Have you said yes to God's invitation? If not, what is holding you back? Who can you talk to this week about taking this step and assuring your place in Heaven with God?

_____

_____

_____

_____

_____

_____

_____

_____

_____

_____

_____

_____

Day 7 – Heaven on Earth

The New Jerusalem, which is in Heaven, will come down to the New Earth where God will dwell with his redeemed people on Earth.

> *And I saw the holy city, the New Jerusalem, coming down from God out of heaven like a bride beautifully dressed for her husband.* [3]*I heard a loud shout from the throne, saying, "Look, God's home is now among his people! He will live with them, and they will be his people. God himself will be with them.* Revelation 21:2–3 (NLT)

Reflection: What do you think about living on a New Earth that is also Heaven?

_____

_____

_____

_____

_____

_____

_____

_____

_____

_____

_____

_____

_____

SESSION 2: THE PRESENT HEAVEN

Memory Verse: *...today you will be with me in Paradise.* Luke 23:43 (NIV)

In our last session we talked about the misconception shared by many people that Heaven is where all people go when they die. Another common misconception is the belief that the place where we go when we die is our final destination. This session helps us understand where people go when they die, God's plan for the future, and what that means for us.

Open your group with prayer.

CONNECTING WITH GOD'S FAMILY (10 MIN)

1. If anyone new has joined your group this week, take a few minutes to briefly introduce yourselves.

2. Briefly discuss how you feel knowing that Heaven is not mankind's default destination.

3. Theologians describe the place we go when we die as an Intermediate Heaven. How has the knowledge that the current, intermediate, Heaven is not the final destination of believers affected you?

Watch the DVD teaching for this session now. After watching the video, have someone read the discussion questions in the *Growing* section and direct the group discussion.

GROWING TO BE LIKE CHRIST (30 MIN)

In the last session, we looked at Luke 23:43 and learned that believers go to Paradise, or the Intermediate Heaven, when they die. In today's teaching, Randy explained that Paradise is Heaven, but not the eternal Heaven. Paradise is an Intermediate Heaven where believers wait in anticipation for the New Earth where God's children will live together with the Lord in resurrected bodies for all eternity.

4. Although the Intermediate Heaven is NOT an eternal Heaven, we can be confident in the promise of the resurrection and eternal life (*Heaven*, p. 41–43).

    ...since death came through a man [Adam], the resurrection of the dead comes also through a man [Jesus]. ²²For as in Adam all die, so <u>in Christ all will be made alive</u>. ²³But each in his own turn: Christ, the firstfruits; then, <u>when he comes</u>, those who belong to him. 1 Corinthians 15:21–23 (NIV)

    What do you see in 1 Corinthians 15:21–23 that indicates believers in Christ will indeed be resurrected from the dead?

    When will the resurrection occur according to this passage?

5. *But in keeping with his promise we are looking forward to a new heaven and a new earth, the home of righteousness.* 2 Peter 3:13 (NIV)

    Scripture tells us that the New Earth will be a *real place* where believers will live together with the Lord in resurrected bodies for all eternity (*Heaven*, p. 44). What does 2 Peter 3:13 say about what we should be doing as we wait on God's timing?

6. *Meanwhile we groan, longing to be clothed with our heavenly dwelling, because when we are clothed, we will not be found naked. For while we are in this tent, we groan and are burdened, because we do not wish to be unclothed but to be clothed with our heavenly dwelling, so that what is mortal may be swallowed up by life.* 2 Corinthians 5:2–4 (NIV)

Paul said in Philippians 1:22–24, *If I am to go on living in the body, this will mean fruitful labor for me. Yet what shall I choose? I do not know!* ²³*I am torn between the two: I desire to depart and be with Christ, which is better by far;* ²⁴*but it is more necessary for you that I remain in the body.* (NIV)

What do you think Paul is implying about the state of our bodies after we die? (*Heaven*, p. 57–59)

7. Scripture provides a wealth of insight into life in Heaven. From the following verses, what do you observe that gives us a glimpse into what life will be like in Heaven? Discuss your observations of each passage and make notes in the space to the right, if desired.

Passage for Discussion	Notes
The Martyrs for Christ: ...*called out in a loud voice, "How long, Sovereign Lord, holy and true, until you judge the inhabitants of the earth and avenge our blood?"* Revelation 6:10	
It is written: "As surely as I live," says the Lord, *"every knee will bow before me; every tongue will confess to God."* ¹²*So then, each of us will give an account of himself to God.* Romans 14:11–12 (NIV)	
And there was given to each of them a white robe; and they were told that they should rest for a little while longer, until the number of their fellow servants and their brethren who were to be killed even as they had been, would be completed also. Revelation 6:11 (NASB)	
"I tell you that in the same way, there will be more joy in heaven over one sinner who repents than over ninety-nine righteous persons who need no repentance." Luke 15:7 (NASB)	

Passage for Discussion	Notes
They will not toil in vain or bear children doomed to misfortune; for they will be a people blessed by the Lord, they and their descendants with them. Isaiah 65:23 (NIV)	

8. *...there shall certainly be a resurrection of both the righteous and the wicked.* Acts 24:15b (NASB)

   What does Acts 24:15b tell us about who will be resurrected from the dead?

   John wrote in Revelation verses 20:12 and 15, *And I saw the dead, great and small, standing before the throne, and books were opened. Another book was opened, which is the book of life. The dead were judged according to what they had done as recorded in the books. ...¹⁵If anyone's name was not found written in the book of life, he was thrown into the lake of fire.* (NIV)

   Philippians 4:3 indicates that the names of believers are written in the Book of Life. What does Revelation 20:15 say about the destination of unbelievers? (*Heaven*, p. 24–27)

9. We need assurance that our names are written in the Book of Life. *Jesus [said], "I am the way and the truth and the life. No one comes to the Father except through me."* John 14:6 (NIV)

   But what does it say? "The word is near you; it is in your mouth and in your heart," that is, the word of faith we are proclaiming: ⁹That if you confess with your mouth, "Jesus is Lord," and believe in your heart that God raised him from the dead, you will be saved. ¹⁰For it is with your heart that you believe and are justified, and it is with your mouth that you confess and are saved. Romans 10:8–10 (NLT)

   What do we learn about spending eternity with God in John 14:6 and Romans 10:8–10? (*Heaven*, p. 33–36)

10. 1 Peter 3:11–14 gives us insight into how we can be ready for Heaven.

> *Since everything around us is going to be destroyed like this, what holy and godly lives you should live,* ¹²*<u>looking forward to the day of God and hurrying it along</u>. On that day, he will set the Heavens on fire, and the elements will melt away in the flames.* ¹³*But we are looking forward to the new Heavens and new earth he has promised, a world filled with God's righteousness.*

> ¹⁴*And so, dear friends, <u>while you are waiting</u> for these things to happen, make every effort to be found living peaceful lives that are pure and blameless in his sight.* (NLT)

What do these passages say about how we should live while we're here on earth? (*Heaven*, p. 471–472)

11. *But store up for yourselves treasures in heaven, where neither moth nor rust destroys, and where thieves do not break in or steal;* ²¹*for where your treasure is, there your heart will be also.* Matthew 6:20–21 (NASB)

Discuss what you think "treasures" refers to in this passage? What do you think Jesus meant when he said *"where your treasure is, there your heart will be"*? (*Heaven*, pp. 340, 370–371, 471–472)

12. *But these are written that you may believe that Jesus is the Christ, the Son of God, and that by believing you may have life in his name.* John 20:31 (NLT)

I write these things to you who believe in the name of the Son of God so that you may know that you have eternal life. 1 John 5:13 (NLT)

How important are these words to you personally? Are you certain that you are ready for Heaven? If not, discuss this with the group now or with your leader after the group time today.

DEVELOPING YOUR GIFTS TO SERVE OTHERS (15 MIN)

"Christ-centered righteous living today is directly affected by knowing where we're going and what rewards we'll receive there for serving Christ. After all, if we really believe we're going to live forever in a realm where Christ is the center of our greatest joy, and that righteous living will mean happiness for all, why wouldn't we choose to get a head start on Heaven through Christ-centered righteous living now?" (*Heaven*, pp. 470–471)

13. Most people want to live a healthy, balanced life, and *knowing* where we are headed for eternity can directly affect how we live today. The *Personal Health Assessment* on pages 112–113 in the *Appendix* is a great starting place for evaluating how you are doing spiritually. Take a few minutes to individually complete your assessments now. This is not a test and is only intended to help you identify some areas where you would like to grow. You won't be asked to share your results with the group.

14. Following through with plans and commitments can be tough on our own, but it becomes easier when we are accountable to a friend. Connect with someone in your group to share your thoughts with during this study. (We suggest that men partner with men and women with women.)

    On page 111 in the *Appendix* you will find a *Personal Health Plan*, a chart for keeping track of your spiritual progress throughout this study. In the box that says, "WHO are you connecting with spiritually?" write your partner's name. In the box that says, "WHAT is your next step for growth?" write one step you would like to take for growth during this study. Look back at your *Personal Health Assessment* for ideas.

    Share with your partner a next step you are choosing to take. For now, don't worry about the WHERE, WHEN, and HOW questions on the *Personal Health Plan*.

PRAYER AND SURRENDER (10 MIN)

15. This session has helped us understand more about what happens when people die, what Heaven is like, and what is required to assure that we will go to Heaven when we die. Take a few minutes now to pray together for your response to the ideas presented in this session. Ask God to help you understand what he wants you to do in response to what you have learned and to help you find answers to any questions you still have regarding what Heaven is really like and what it takes to get there.

16. Take a few minutes to share prayer requests and praises in the group. Record the requests and praises on the *Prayer and Praise Report* beginning on page 123 to use as a reminder to pray for group members throughout the next week.

17. Talk together about what it would take to make time with God a priority every day or even five or six days a week. Consider drawing near to God for a few minutes each day; gradually you will desire more. Use the *Reflections* at the end of the session for focusing on the principles of this study as you spend time with God each day.

> **Note:** We suggest you read *Days 8* through *14* in the *50 Days of Heaven* book as you work through the *Reflections*. If you don't have time to work through all the *Reflections* before your next group meeting, we suggest you work through the day(s) marked with an asterisk.

SCRIPTURE STUDY

If you want to dig deeper into the Bible passages about the topic at hand, we've provided suggested study passages below. The *Growing* section provides you with plenty to discuss within the group, so we recommend that participants study these passages on their own between group meetings, if desired.

- 1 Corinthians 3:12–15; 4:9; 15:44
- 2 Corinthians 5: 8, 10
- 1 John 3:8
- 1 Samuel 28:3–8, 16–19
- 1 Thessalonians 4:13–14
- 1 Timothy 3:16; 5:21; 6:19
- 2 Timothy 2:5
- 2 Kings 6:17; 19:15
- 2 Peter 3
- Acts 7:55–56
- Daniel 12:2–3
- Ecclesiastes 12:7
- Ephesians 1:10; 3:15
- Ezekiel 28:13
- Genesis 1–2; 3:8, 17, 24
- Hebrews 12:1
- Isaiah 65:17; 66:22
- James 5:16
- John 14:2–3
- Luke 9:31; 12:33; 15: 7, 10; 16:22–31; 19:17; 23:43
- Malachi 3:16
- Matthew 6:19–21; 12:36; 19:21
- Philippians 1:23
- Psalm 24:1
- Revelation 2–3; 5:8; 6; 14:13; 18; 20–22
- Romans 8:34

REFLECTIONS

Each day, read a *Reflection* below, giving prayerful consideration to what you learn about God, his Spirit, and his place in your life. If you don't have time to work through all the *Reflections* before your next group meeting, we suggest you work through the day(s) marked with an asterisk.

Use the space included for each day to write down any thoughts or feelings that God is putting on your heart.

Day 8 – Where God's People Go When They Die

When we leave earth and enter into the presence of God, we will be home. We have hope of a wonderful eternity after this life. For now we look forward to living with God in the Intermediate Heaven with anticipation of living with him eternally in the New Heaven on the New Earth.

> *And now, dear brothers and sisters, we want you to know what will happen to the believers who have died so you will not grieve like people who have no hope.*
> 1 Thessalonians 4:13 (NLT)

Reflection: The idea of an Intermediate Heaven may be new to you; consider what you've learned about the Intermediate Heaven this week. Ask God to show you what he wants you to focus on.

_____

_____

_____

_____

_____

_____

Day 9 – The Present (Intermediate) Heaven: A Physical Place?

In Acts 7:55–56, Stephen saw things that were described as being real and physical. Heaven is a real and a physical place.

> *But Stephen, full of the Holy Spirit, gazed steadily into heaven and saw the glory of God, and he saw Jesus standing in the place of honor at God's right hand.* [56] *And he told them, "Look, I see the heavens opened and the Son of Man standing in the place of honor at God's right hand!"* Acts 7:55–56 (NLT)

Reflection: Think about Heaven as a real place. How does this help you look forward to Heaven?

_____

_____

_____

_____

_____

_____

_____

_____

_____

_____

_____

_____

_____

_____

Day 10 – Paradise: The Present Heaven

Jesus assured the thief, hanging on the cross next to him that he would be with him that day in Paradise. Jesus was speaking of the place we go when we leave this earth, the Intermediate Heaven. The Garden of Eden was not destroyed when Adam and Eve were removed from it and it is the place where the Tree of Life remains. The Paradise Jesus spoke of may be the Garden of Eden and the place we occupy in the Intermediate Heaven.

> *Jesus answered him, "I tell you the truth, today you will be with me in Paradise."* Luke 23:43 (NIV)

Reflection: What do you imagine Paradise to be like? What sounds good to you about the present Heaven right now?

_____

_____

_____

_____

_____

_____

_____

_____

_____

_____

_____

_____

Day 11 – Seeing Earth From Heaven

The Bible gives us a lot of evidence that what goes on here on earth is visible to those in Heaven. If there is rejoicing in Heaven when one sinner comes to Christ, it is clear that those in Heaven are able to see what is happening on earth.

> *I tell you that in the same way there will be more rejoicing in heaven over one sinner who repents than over ninety-nine righteous persons who do not need to repent.* Luke 15:7 (NIV)

Reflection: Who was rejoicing in Heaven when you came to Christ? How does knowing they are there and watching you, help you to press on toward spiritual growth?

_____

_____

_____

_____

_____

_____

_____

_____

_____

_____

_____

_____

_____

Day 12 – Heaven's Inhabitants: Remembering and Praying?

Scripture tells us that when we are in Heaven we will remember what happened to us on earth. We will give an account of our lives and receive our rewards accordingly. We will be united with the saints that went to Heaven before us, and we will know what is happening in the lives of the saints on earth. We will join Jesus in constant prayer for them.

> *For we must all appear before the judgment seat of Christ, so that each one may be recompensed for his deeds in the body, according to what he has done, whether good or bad.* 2 Corinthians 5:10 (NASB)

Reflection: How are you encouraged by knowing where your loved ones are and that one day you'll be with them again in the presence of God?

_____

_____

_____

_____

_____

_____

_____

_____

_____

_____

_____

_____

*Day 13 – God's Plan to Redeem the Earth

In the same way that God promises to redeem and make mankind new, he will also redeem the earth. This promise of a renewed earth, the New Heavens and the New Earth, give us good reason for grateful worship of our Lord.

> *Behold, I will create new heavens and a new earth...* Isaiah 65:17 (NIV)

Reflection: Take time to thank God today for his masterful plan to redeem us and the earth.

_____

_____

_____

_____

_____

_____

_____

_____

_____

_____

_____

_____

_____

_____

Day 14 – The New Earth: A Real Earth?

God made this earth for us, but it has been destroyed by sin. However God will redeem this earth and refashion it into the New Earth, where we will live forever with him. All things were created by God for his glory, and he will not give up on us or his creation.

> And I heard a loud voice from the throne, saying, "Behold, the tabernacle of God is among men, and He will dwell among them, and they shall be His people, and God Himself will be among them, ⁴and He will wipe away every tear from their eyes; and there will no longer be any death; there will no longer be any mourning, or crying, or pain; the first things have passed away." ⁵And He who sits on the throne said, "Behold, I am making all things new." And He said, "Write, for these words are faithful and true." Revelation 21:3–5 (NASB)

Reflection: Reflect on the knowledge that this earth will not remain in its current state forever.

_____

_____

_____

_____

_____

_____

_____

_____

_____

_____

_____

SESSION 3: THE NEW EARTH

Memory Verse: *But in keeping with his promise we are looking forward to a new heaven and a new earth, the home of righteousness.* 2 Peter 3:13 (NIV)

What will the coming renewal of all things include? *Everything.* Everything will be restored, returned to its original condition. Mankind will be *restored* to what we once were, what God designed us to be—fully embodied and righteous beings. The universe—the rest of *everything*—will be restored to what it once was. Can you imagine? God will restore everything *on earth*, just as Acts 3:21 confirms: *For he must remain in heaven until the time for the final restoration of all things, as God promised long ago through his holy prophets.*[1] (NLT)

Open your group with prayer.

 CONNECTING WITH GOD'S FAMILY (10 MIN)

Each of us came to this study with a different personal history and varying thoughts and ideas about Heaven. Sharing a bit of our background can help us get to know one another and bond as a group.

1. If you have any newcomers joining you this week, take a few moments to briefly introduce yourselves.

2. Take turns sharing how your beliefs about Heaven are being challenged or confirmed through this study.

3. In session two you filled in the "WHAT" goal of your *Personal Health Plan.* Pair up with your partner and share how things are going for you in regards to accomplishing the next step you set for yourself last week.

---

[1] Adapted from *50 Days of Heaven: Reflections that Bring Eternity to Light*, Randy Alcorn pages 71–72.

Watch the DVD teaching for this session now. After watching the video, have someone read the discussion questions in the *Growing* section and direct the group discussion.

 GROWING TO BE LIKE CHRIST (30 MIN)

Restoration implies renewal or rebuilding of something that has been damaged or destroyed. In our teaching video today we learned about the importance of Christ's resurrection, how our resurrection affects all of creation, and some things we can expect to find on the New Earth.

4. According to 1 Corinthians 15:12–19, why is Christ's resurrection so important? (*Heaven*, pp. 111, 116–119)

    But if it is preached that Christ has been raised from the dead, how can some of you say that there is no resurrection of the dead? *¹³If there is no resurrection of the dead, then not even Christ has been raised. ¹⁴And if Christ has not been raised, our preaching is useless and so is your faith. ¹⁵More than that, we are then found to be false witnesses about God, for we have testified about God that he raised Christ from the dead. But he did not raise him if in fact the dead are not raised. ¹⁶For if the dead are not raised, then Christ has not been raised either. ¹⁷And if Christ has not been raised, your faith is futile; you are still in your sins. ¹⁸Then those also who have fallen asleep in Christ are lost. ¹⁹If only for this life we have hope in Christ, we are to be pitied more than all men.* 1 Corinthians 15:12–19 (NIV)

5. The following chart outlines Genesis 3:14–19. Review the verses and discuss how all of creation was cursed when Adam and Eve sinned. Make notes in the space provided, if desired. (*Heaven*, pp. 105–107)

Genesis 3 (NLT)	What life is affected?
[14]Then the LORD God said to the serpent, "Because you have done this, you are cursed more than all animals, domestic and wild. You will crawl on your belly, groveling in the dust as long as you live.	
[15]And I will cause hostility between you and the woman, and between your offspring and her offspring. He will strike your head, and you will strike his heel."	
[16]Then he said to the woman, "I will sharpen the pain of your pregnancy, and in pain you will give birth. And you will desire to control your husband, but he will rule over you."	
[17]And to the man he said, "Since you listened to your wife and ate from the tree whose fruit I commanded you not to eat, the ground is cursed because of you. All your life you will struggle to scratch a living from it. [18]It will grow thorns and thistles for you, though you will eat of its grains.	
[19]By the sweat of your brow will you have food to eat until you return to the ground from which you were made. For you were made from dust, and to dust you will return."	

What changed on earth because of the sin of Adam and Eve?

6. The Garden of Eden was created by God to be an eternally perfect place for perfect people to live forever. When Adam

and Eve sinned, creation moved from eternal perfection into death and decay. This death was spiritual since they were put out of fellowship with God, but it was also physical. Although Adam and Eve did not die immediately, they eventually did die physically. However God will fulfill his original intention for us and creation.

So you see, just as death came into the world through a man, now the resurrection from the dead has begun through another man [Jesus]. ²²Just as everyone dies because we all belong to Adam, everyone who belongs to Christ will be given new life. ²³But there is an order to this resurrection: Christ was raised as the first of the harvest; then all who belong to Christ will be raised when he comes back. 1 Corinthians 15:21–23 (NLT)

How does 1 Corinthians 15:21–23 reveal God's plan to fulfill his original intentions for us? (*Heaven*, pp. 112–113)

7. All creation will reap the results of our resurrection. What does Romans 8:19–21 say about how God will fulfill his original intentions for all of creation?

    The creation waits in eager expectation for the sons of God to be revealed. ²⁰For the creation was subjected to frustration, not by its own choice, but by the will of the one who subjected it, in hope ²¹that the creation itself will be liberated from its bondage to decay and brought into the glorious freedom of the children of God. Romans 8:19–21 (NIV)

8. What's going to prevent another fall from happening in eternity?

    The Bible says, *the wages of sin is death* (Romans 6:23). What promise do we see in Revelation 21:4 that answers the question of a future fall?

    He will wipe every tear from their eyes. There will be no more death or mourning or crying or pain, for the old order of things has passed away. Revelation 21:4 (NIV)

9. *For since the creation of the world God's invisible qualities—his eternal power and divine nature—have been clearly seen, being understood from what has been made, so that men are without excuse.* Romans 1:20 (NIV)

On the New Earth we will see the natural beauty of this world as God always intended it to be. There will be no more pollution and misuse of creation, something we have never experienced. How do you see God's invisible qualities presently on earth? In what ways is seeing him in creation meaningful to you? (*Heaven*, p. 175)

10. This world is a shadow of what we'll one day experience on the New Earth. What are you looking forward to most as you anticipate the New Earth? (*Heaven*, pp. 107–108, 175–178)

11. From what we have studied today about the resurrection of Christ, the resurrection of mankind, and the renewal of all things—including all of creation—how do you see that God is glorified in all or part of it?

In what ways does your life glorify God? If you have a hard time answering this, discuss some practical ways we can glorify God in our daily lives.

 SHARING YOUR LIFE MISSION EVERY DAY (10 MIN)

Many people refuse to talk about what happens to us after we die. Maybe you know someone like that. A study like this can offer people hope, security, and release from fear of the unknown, if we are willing to share with them.

12.	In the first session we asked you to identify on the *Circles of Life* diagram (page 11) some people to invite to your group. Share how your invitations went.

   If you haven't followed through, think about what is preventing you from doing it. As a group, consider some ways to overcome obstacles or excuses that keep us from reaching out and inviting people into the group.

 PRAYER AND SURRENDER (10 MIN)

Praying together builds your connection with one another. A study like this one will raise different feelings in each of us.

13.	As a group, pray for God to reveal what we have to look forward to beyond our life here on earth. Ask him to remind you that he is with you every moment. Pray that daily you can recognize him and see his creation as a promise of what awaits you after the resurrection of believers.

14.	Share prayer requests in your group and record the requests and praises on the *Prayer and Praise Report* beginning on page 123. Commit to praying for each other throughout the week between group meetings. The *Prayer and Praise Report* can be a reminder of what to pray for group members over the next week.

Note: We suggest you read *Days 15* through *21* in the *50 Days of Heaven* book as you work through the *Reflections*. If you don't have time to work through all the *Reflections* before your next group meeting, we suggest you work through the day(s) marked with an asterisk.

SCRIPTURE STUDY

If you want to dig deeper into the Bible passages about the topic at hand, we've provided suggested study passages below. The *Growing* section provides you with plenty to discuss within the group, so we recommend that participants study these passages on their own between group meetings, if desired.

- 1 Corinthians 15:17–19, 22, 42–44, 49, 53
- 1 John 3:21
- 1 Thessalonians 4:14, 17
- 2 Corinthians 5:17
- Acts 3:21; 9:3–9
- Colossians 1:16–20
- Daniel 12:3
- Ecclesiastes 3:11
- Ephesians 1:10
- Ezekiel 43:2
- Genesis 1:28; 3:17–22; 9:1
- Isaiah 2:12–13, 16–19; 10:34; 11:9–10; 40:5; 52–53; 60; 66:19–20
- Job 19:26–27
- John 2:19–21; 20:15, 19; 21:4–5, 12
- Luke 2:38; Luke 9:29–31; 24:13–35, 39
- Matthew 13:43; 19:28
- Numbers 14:21
- Philippians 3:20–21
- Psalm 46:1–3; 85:9; 102:15–16
- Revelation 6:15; 21–23–26
- Romans 5:15–19; 8:2, 19–23

REFLECTIONS

Each day, read a *Reflection* below, giving prayerful consideration to what you learn about God, his Spirit, and his place in your life. If you don't have time to work through all the *Reflections* before your next group meeting, we suggest you work through the day(s) marked with an asterisk.

*Day 15 – The Coming "Renewal of All Things"

The Lord will restore all things to what he originally intended them to be. Just as we look forward to our redemption in Christ, all creation looks forward to being renewed as well. This will be a new beginning, a new genesis, a coming back from death to life.

> *Jesus said to them, "I tell you the truth, at the renewal of all things, when the Son of Man sits on his glorious throne, you who have followed me will also sit on twelve thrones, judging the twelve tribes of Israel.* Matthew 19:28 (NIV)

Reflection: God's stated purpose for us is to rule over the earth forever. In the end Christ will renew all things. How do these truths help you face the challenges of today?

_____

_____

_____

_____

_____

_____

_____

Day 16 – A Vision of the New Earth

The words of Isaiah 60 describe the New Earth with the very same words as Revelation 21–22. These verses speak of unprecedented rejoicing, *"Then you will look and be radiant, your heart will throb and swell with joy."*

> *Your gates will always stand open, they will never be shut, day or night, so that men may bring you the wealth of the nations—their kings led in triumphal procession* [15]*...I will make you the everlasting pride and the joy of all generations.* Isaiah 60:11, 15 (NIV)

Reflection: Our days on earth are often burdened with troubles and frustrations but seeing a vision of the New Earth can encourage us while we finish our days here. What aspect of the New Earth can you focus on to encourage you in the midst of your daily circumstances?

_____

_____

_____

_____

_____

_____

_____

_____

_____

_____

_____

_____

Day 17 – God's Glory on God's Earth

All creation is under the curse, yet the Lord said, *The glory of the Lord fills the whole earth* (Numbers 14:21). God's glorious display will be even greater after the redemption of all creation. *And the glory of the LORD will be revealed, and all mankind together will see it. For the mouth of the LORD has spoken.* Isaiah 40:5 and Isaiah 11:9–10 speak of how glorious it will be when the nations rally to the LORD at his holy mountain.

> *They will neither harm nor destroy on all my holy mountain, for the earth will be full of the knowledge of the LORD as the waters cover the sea.* ¹⁰*In that day the Root of Jesse will stand as a banner for the peoples; the nations will rally to him, and his place of rest will be glorious.* Isaiah 11:9–10 (NIV)

Reflection: When you think of God's glory on earth, what do you envision? How do you think seeing the glory of the Lord will change your experience with him?

_____

_____

_____

_____

_____

_____

_____

_____

_____

_____

_____

Day 18 – The Curse Reversed

The cross and the resurrection of Jesus make the restoration of mankind and all of creation possible. Just as in Christ we are reconciled to God because he reversed the curse, God will also redeem the whole earth and all of creation according to Romans 8:18–19, *I consider that our present sufferings are not worth comparing with the glory that will be revealed in us. ¹⁹The creation waits in eager expectation for the sons of God to be revealed.*

> *No longer will there be any curse.* Revelation 22:3 (NIV)

Reflection: What aspect of the curse being reversed means the most to you and why?

_____

_____

_____

_____

_____

_____

_____

_____

_____

_____

_____

_____

_____

Day 19 – Our Old Bodies Made New

First Corinthians 15:53 tells us that we, being perishable, must put on immortality. This speaks of our bodies being made new, becoming immortal. But it doesn't mean that we are not the very same people who will also walk the New Earth.

> *For the perishable must clothe itself with the imperishable, and the mortal with immortality.* 1 Corinthians 15:53 (NIV)

Reflection: As you think about the resurrection and our bodies being made imperishable, what changes do you consider to be most exciting or that you most look forward to personally experiencing?

_____

_____

_____

_____

_____

_____

_____

_____

_____

_____

_____

_____

Day 20 – Christ's Resurrection Body: The Model for Ours

God promises us new resurrected bodies when Christ returns because of the work he did on the cross in our place. Christ's resurrection is the prototype for the resurrection of mankind and the earth.

> *But our citizenship is in heaven. And we eagerly await a Savior from there, the Lord Jesus Christ, [21] who, by the power that enables him to bring everything under his control, will transform our lowly bodies so that they will be like his glorious body.* Philippians 3:20–21 (NIV)

Reflection: How is your view of your future body affected by Christ's bodily resurrection? What do you think life on the New Earth will be like based on your view of Christ's bodily resurrection?

_____

_____

_____

_____

_____

_____

_____

_____

_____

_____

_____

_____

Day 21 – As Mankind Goes, So Goes Creation

Creation waits eagerly upon our resurrection for deliverance. The glorification of the universe hinges on the glorification of a redeemed human race.

> *The creation waits in eager expectation for the sons of God to be revealed. [20]For the creation was subjected to frustration, not by its own choice, but by the will of the one who subjected it, in hope [21]that the creation itself will be liberated from its bondage to decay and brought into the glorious freedom of the children of God.*
>
> *[22]We know that the whole creation has been groaning as in the pains of childbirth right up to the present time. [23]Not only so, but we ourselves, who have the firstfruits of the Spirit, groan inwardly as we wait eagerly for our adoption as sons, the redemption of our bodies.* Romans 8:19–23 (NIV)

Reflection: What do you see in creation or within yourself that is evidence that creation is groaning for something better? If you can identify one or two things you long for, what are they?

_____

_____

_____

_____

_____

_____

_____

_____

_____

_____

SESSION 4: REIGNING AND RULING

Memory Verse: *Here is a trustworthy saying: If we died with him, we will also live with him;* [12]*if we endure, we will also reign with him.* 2 Timothy 2:11–12a (NIV)

C.S. Lewis said, "If I find in myself a desire which no experience in this world can satisfy, the most probable explanation is that I was made for another world."[1]

Haven't we all felt out of place at times, even when things seem to be going well? This is because things are not currently what God originally intended them to be. But the perfect earth is coming and Jesus Christ is going to be the King of kings over the New Earth. We will reign with him over the earth, kings and queens under him, stewarding his creation for eternity.

Open your group with prayer.

 CONNECTING WITH GOD'S FAMILY (5 MIN)

The Bible says we will actually reign with Christ. Ruling may not sound like Heaven—the leadership that is required may seem too much like work. But from God's perspective, leadership is about serving, and service is a reward, not a punishment.

1. Talk about what you think ruling with Christ will look like. What skills and abilities do you have that might be utilized in the New Earth?

Watch the DVD teaching for this session now. After watching the video, have someone read the discussion questions in the *Growing* section and direct the group discussion.

---

[1] Lewis, C. S., *Mere Christianity*, 120.

GROWING TO BE LIKE CHRIST (30 MIN)

Most people do not feel satisfied and fulfilled no matter how much they have or how busy they are. That's because God designed us for something more—a better world.

2. Second Peter 3:13 says, *But in keeping with his promise we are looking forward to a new heaven and a new earth, the home of righteousness* (NIV).

   For this world is not our permanent home; we are looking forward to a home yet to come. Hebrews 13:14 (NLT)

   These verses tell us that, by nature, we look forward to something more than life on this earth has to offer (*Heaven*, pp. 77–78). Think about your own longings for Heaven. How did you picture Heaven prior to this study? Discuss how your perspective has changed since beginning this study.

3. This world is not perfect; nor will we see all God has planned for us here. What does Hebrews 11:39–40 say that helps us understand what God has planned for his people?

   All these people earned a good reputation because of their faith, yet none of them received all that God had promised. [40]For God had something better in mind for us... Hebrews 11:39–40a (NLT)

   In light of our study so far, what do you think this passage is referring to?

4. Daniel, interpreting King Nebuchadnezzar's dream, said to him, *But after your kingdom comes to an end, another great kingdom, inferior to yours, will rise to take your place. After that kingdom has fallen, yet a third great kingdom, represented by the bronze belly and thighs, will rise to rule the world. [40]Following that kingdom, there will be a fourth great kingdom, as strong as iron. That kingdom will smash and crush all previous empires, just as iron smashes and crushes everything it strikes. [41]The feet and toes you saw that were a combination of iron and clay show that this kingdom will be divided. [42]Some parts of it will be as strong as*

iron, and others as weak as clay. ⁴³This mixture of iron and clay also shows that these kingdoms will try to strengthen themselves by forming alliances with each other through intermarriage. But this will not succeed, just as iron and clay do not mix. ⁴⁴During the reigns of those kings, the God of heaven will set up a kingdom that will never be destroyed or conquered. It will crush all these kingdoms into nothingness, and it will stand forever. Daniel 2:39–44 (NLT)

What does this passage say about the fate of the kingdoms of men? Verse 44 speaks about a kingdom that will come down and will never be destroyed. What kingdom do you understand this to be? (*Heaven,* pp. 228–231)

5. Second Timothy 2:11–12a says that the faithful will reign with Christ. *Here is a trustworthy saying: If we died with him, we will also live with him; ¹²if we endure, we will also reign with him.* 2 Timothy 2:11–12a (NIV)

What is required to reign with Christ forever according to 2 Timothy 2:11–12?

Read Revelation 4:4 together aloud. *Surrounding the throne were twenty-four other thrones, and seated on them were twenty-four elders. They were dressed in white and had crowns of gold on their heads.* Revelation 4:4 (NIV)

What do you think the thrones and crowns in this verse represent?

What do these verses say to you about God's desire to reward his people? (*Heaven,* pp. 233–235)

6. Today, we don't see the kind of rule over the earth spoken of in Genesis 1:26. *Then God said, "Let us make man in our image, in our likeness, and let them rule over the fish of the sea and the birds of the air, over the livestock, over all the earth, and over all the creatures that move along the ground." Genesis 1:26.*

    What do you think God meant when he said that he made man to rule over all the earth? (*Heaven*, pp. 226–227)

7. As we listened to Randy Alcorn talk about the New Earth and ruling and reigning over it, what kind of culture do you imagine believers will live in on the New Earth?

8. Most people probably don't picture themselves working in Heaven. How do you feel about Randy Alcorn's teaching that we will work in Heaven? (*Heaven*, pp. 411–414)

    What did Randy say that resonated with you? Why?

9. Immanuel means God with us. Randy Alcorn said that Jesus' incarnation is eternal, not temporary. He was made for earth and he will dwell on the earth forever as King of kings in the New Jerusalem. (*Heaven*, pp. 93–95, 149)

    What about his physical presence with us are you looking forward to? Consider John 14:9 for insight.

10. *But Jesus called [his disciples] to Himself and said, "You know that the rulers of the Gentiles lord it over them, and their great men exercise authority over them. ²⁶It is not this way among you, but whoever wishes to become great among you shall be your servant..."* Matthew 20:25–26 (NASB)

What does Matthew 20:25–26 say about the role of the servant?

11. In his teaching today, Randy spoke of a bellman he met who faithfully served others while viewing himself as unworthy even to receive a gift—he was "only a bellman." But Randy was struck by how different this servant's role could be in Heaven.

    Do you see yourself as a ruler or a servant today? What would it take for you to view yourself as the servant that God wants you to be? (*Heaven*, p. 235)

 DEVELOPING YOUR GIFTS TO SERVE OTHERS (15 MIN)

Our study this week has expanded our awareness of what we will do when Heaven is relocated to the New Earth. We will be ruling and reigning with Jesus, we will be given work to do, and we will carry it all out joyfully.

12. Our small group presents an opportunity to begin the kind of service that prepares us for what we might do in Heaven. We suggest each of you take on a small role within your group for the next few weeks. This will build group commitment and a sense of belonging. See the box titled *Group Member Roles* on the next page for ideas.

    What small commitment will you take on within the group? Spend some time now discussing your group needs and who might fill them.

13. In your *Personal Health Plan* on page 111, next to the "Develop" icon, answer the "WHERE" are you serving?" question. Also note a next step you can take to better serve in your small group or church community. If you are not currently serving, note how

you will begin. Share your next step with your spiritual partner and tell him/her how to pray for you.

PRAYER AND SURRENDER (10 MIN)

14. Take a few minutes to share your prayer requests. We recommend using the *Prayer and Praise Report* beginning on page 123 to record requests and answers to prayer each week. This practice will help you remember how to pray for group members between group meetings.

15. Break into small groups of two to four people and pray together now. Thank God for the hope we have in reigning and ruling with him in Heaven forever. Ask him to develop a servant's heart in each of you and to show you how to serve as Jesus served.

Group Member Roles

Coordinate socials and group celebrations (birthdays, dinners, and group activities).

Follow up on new and absent people with calls and cards.

Encourage people to bring their friends.

Encourage people to complete the *Health Assessment* and *Health Plan*.

Encourage every member to establish a daily quiet time.

Help each member discover his/her personal ministry in the church.

Encourage prayer for unchurched friends or family members.

Pray for service opportunities and plan short-term outreach projects.

Lead the group prayer time.

Coordinate a weekly prayer and praise list by email.

Coordinate your group attending church services together. (Encourage people to attend in sub-groups of 2–4, if not all together.)

Host a simple worship time for your small group

Note: We suggest you read *Days 22* through *28* in the *50 Days of Heaven* book as you work through the *Reflections*. If you don't have time to work through all the *Reflections* before your next group meeting, we suggest you work through the day(s) marked with an asterisk.

SCRIPTURE STUDY

If you want to dig deeper into the Bible passages about the topic at hand, we've provided suggested study passages below. The *Growing* section provides you with plenty to discuss within the group, so we recommend that participants study these passages on their own between group meetings, if desired.

- 1 Corinthians 6:2–3
- 1 Peter 3; 5:5–6
- 2 Corinthians 5:8, 17; 6:16
- 2 Peter 3:13
- 2 Timothy 2:12; 4:8
- Daniel 2:44; 7:14; 12:2–3, 13
- Ephesians 6:8
- Ezekiel 37:27
- Genesis 1:1, 28; 3:8
- Hebrews 11:13–14, 16
- Isaiah 9:7; 65, 66
- John 14:3; 17:24
- Leviticus 26:11–12
- Luke 14:11; 16:10; 19:17; 22:29–30
- Matthew 5:3, 5, 10, 12; 21:5; 25:21
- Philippians 1:23
- Proverbs 2:21–22, 10:30
- Psalm 8:6; 37:9–11; 72:8, 11
- Revelation 2-5; 3:12, 21; 7:14–15; 19:11–16; 20:1–8; 21; 22:2, 5
- Zechariah 9:9–10; 14:9

REFLECTIONS

Each day, read a *Reflection* below, giving prayerful consideration to what you learn about God, his Spirit, and his place in your life. If you don't have time to work through all the *Reflections* before your next group meeting, we suggest you work through the day(s) marked with an asterisk.

Day 22 – What the "New" in "New Earth" Means

Since God made us for earth he will make our final destination the New Earth. Just as God will make us new in the final resurrection, he will also renew the earth. This New Earth will be just as God *originally* made the earth we live in now. It will be perfect like the Garden of Eden. We will be able to enjoy nature as we've never seen it before, a reflection of God and his glory.

> *Then I saw a new heaven and a new earth, for the first heaven and the first earth had passed away ... ²I saw the Holy City, the new Jerusalem, coming down out of heaven from God...* Revelation 21:1–2 (NIV)

Reflection: People may feel confused about what the term, new earth, means. How would you explain the *New Earth* to someone?

_____

_____

_____

_____

_____

_____

_____

Day 23 – Homesick for Heaven

We all know what it means to be homesick. We want to be where things are comfortable and familiar. Likewise, our longing for Heaven is really a desire for earth as it should be—as God originally intended it to be. This desire is both biblical and right. The place we long for, "an earth where God is fully glorified, is the very place where [we] will live forever."[1]

> *But in keeping with his promise we are looking forward to a new heaven and a new earth, the home of righteousness.* 2 Peter 3:13 (NIV)

Reflection: Have you felt an unexplainable longing that hasn't been fulfilled? Could it be that you are longing for Heaven?

_____

_____

_____

_____

_____

_____

_____

_____

_____

_____

_____

_____

_____

---

[1] Alcorn, *50 Days of Heaven*, page 114.

Day 24 – The Joy of Living with God Forever

The Scripture is clear that God will dwell with us in Heaven on the New Earth. We won't just *see* him; he will actually walk with us, implying relationship and interaction with him. In John 17:24 Jesus prayed, *"Father, I want those you have given me to be with me where I am ..."* Jesus wants us with him; how wonderful it is to be wanted by our Savior. Think of it, God will be the most important and most fascinating person we'll ever meet in Heaven and we can get to know him here and now.

> *I will put my dwelling place among you ... I will walk among you and be your God, and you will be my people.* Leviticus 26:11–12 (NIV)

Reflection: We can get to know God now by developing our relationship with him. What are you doing to get to know God better? What else can you do?

_____

_____

_____

_____

_____

_____

_____

_____

_____

_____

_____

_____

Day 25 – Promised Land, Promised Earth: The New Earth vs. The Millennium

Scripture is loaded with promises and glimpses of our place, dwelling, and role in eternity. In Jesus' day, the thing that thrilled expectant believers was their hope that one day God would rule on the earth. The millennium question relates to whether the old earth will end soon after Christ returns, or a thousand years later. Regardless, when the old earth ends, the New Earth will begin and last forever. This is the believer's inheritance.

> *For evildoers shall be cut off; But those who wait on the LORD, They shall inherit the earth... [11]But the meek shall inherit the earth, And shall delight themselves in the abundance of peace.* Psalm 37:10–11 (NKJV)

Reflection: How does the promise of an imperishable inheritance on the New Earth give you hope for the future?

_____

_____

_____

_____

_____

_____

_____

_____

_____

_____

_____

_____

Day 26 – The Kingdom of Kingdoms

God created Adam and Eve to rule over the earth, but because of their failure Jesus came as a man and became the new head of the human race. Christ will accomplish what Adam and Eve couldn't. He will rule with his beloved people as his bride and co-rulers. God's desire is to prepare us now for what we will do forever with him.

> *He was given authority, glory and sovereign power; all peoples, nations and men of every language worshiped him. His dominion is an everlasting dominion that will not pass away, and his kingdom is one that will never be destroyed.*
> Daniel 7:14 (NIV)

Reflection: What are you doing to get ready to rule the New Earth? God wants to train you and teach you to lean on his strength and wisdom. How are you cooperating with God's plan?

_____

_____

_____

_____

_____

_____

_____

_____

_____

_____

_____

Day 27 – A Government We'll Love To Be A Part Of

Those with the greatest responsibility in the New Earth will be those who served Christ well with humility on earth. Because we've been conditioned to be skeptical of government as being corrupt and inefficient, we tend to view them with distrust. But in the New Earth we will no longer be skeptical and disillusioned because we will be governed by Christ-like rulers under the gracious governing of Christ himself.

> *And I confer on you a kingdom, just as my Father conferred one on me,* [30]*so that you may eat and drink at my table in my kingdom and sit on thrones, judging the twelve tribes of Israel.* Luke 22:29–30 (NIV)

Reflection: How do you think Christ's rule in Heaven will be different than his rule today? What do you most look forward to on the New Earth under Christ's rule?

_____

_____

_____

_____

_____

_____

_____

_____

_____

_____

_____

_____

*Day 28 – Where Bellmen and Cleaning Ladies Will Rule

Ruling and reigning may not sound appealing at first, especially if you dislike your work. You may think that ruling doesn't sound like Heaven. From God's perspective leadership is about serving, and service is a reward, not a punishment. The more we serve Christ now, the greater our capacity will be to serve him in Heaven.

> *"God opposes the proud but gives grace to the humble."* *⁶Humble yourselves, therefore, under God's mighty hand, that he may lift you up in due time.* 1 Peter 5:5–6 (NIV)

Reflection: Who do you know that exemplifies humble service? How do the actions of the person reveal their humility? What are your thoughts about the humble servants of Christ being lifted up in the eternal kingdom?

_____

_____

_____

_____

_____

_____

_____

_____

_____

_____

_____

SESSION 5: GLIMPSES INTO HEAVEN

Memory Verse: *And he who sits on the throne said, "Behold, I am making all things new."* Revelation 21:5 (NASB)

No doubt our God is creative. Just look at the world around us. There are over 4,600 recognized species of mammals alone, not to mention the countless numbers of other animals, plants, and insects that span the globe. There are majestic mountains, soaring waterfalls, gorgeous desert sunsets, and oceans teeming with vibrant life. Some people might even refer to a few places on this earth as "Paradise," but no matter how beautiful this world is, it remains just a shadow of what is to come on the New Earth.

Many of us wonder what Heaven, or the New Earth, will look like. Will there be mountains, lakes, and deserts? Will there be animals? Some may ask, "Will we be the same people?" or "Will we eat and drink?" During this session, Randy Alcorn addresses these and other questions about life on God's New Earth.

Open your group with prayer.

CONNECTING WITH GOD'S FAMILY (10 MIN)

1. Describe how you imagine God's creation might have been before sin entered the world.

2. Take a few minutes to discuss the future of your group. How many of you are willing to stay together as a group and work through another study? If you have time, review the *Group Values* on page 7 and talk about any changes you would like to make as you move forward as a group.

Watch the DVD teaching for this session now. After watching the video, have someone read the discussion questions in the *Growing* section and direct the group discussion.

Since Adam and Eve's original sin, all of creation has been living under a "curse." But God has promised us *new heavens and a new earth* upon which we will live without sin in the perfect creation that he intended for us since the beginning.

3.   As Randy opened the video teaching, he explained that "curse" is the word theologians use to describe the fallen state of creation that occurred when Adam and Eve first chose the path of sin. Please read Genesis 3:16–19 below. How does this passage describe the curse? Discuss how this description of the curse correlates with how we (God's animate and inanimate creation) experience the effects of the curse today.

To the woman he said, "I will greatly increase your pains in childbearing; with pain you will give birth to children. Your desire will be for your husband, and he will rule over you."

[17]To Adam he said, "Because you listened to your wife and ate from the tree about which I commanded you, 'You must not eat of it,' "Cursed is the ground because of you; through painful toil you will eat of it all the days of your life. [18]It will produce thorns and thistles for you, and you will eat the plants of the field. [19]By the sweat of your brow you will eat your food until you return to the ground, since from it you were taken; for dust you are and to dust you will return." Genesis 3:16–19 (NIV)

4.   Take turns reading the following verses.

Christ redeemed us from the curse of the law by becoming a curse for us, for it is written: "Cursed is everyone who is hung on a tree." Galatians 3:13 (NIV)

And even we Christians, although we have the Holy Spirit within us as a foretaste of future glory, also groan to be released from pain and suffering. We, too, wait anxiously for that day when God will give us our full rights as his children, including the new bodies he has promised us. [24]Now that we are saved, we eagerly look forward to this freedom. For if you already have something, you don't need to hope for it. [25]But if we look forward to something we don't have yet, we must wait patiently and confidently. Romans 8:23–25 (NLT)

How does Galatians 3:13 say mankind is redeemed from the curse? When does this redemption become fully realized according to Romans 8:23? (*Heaven*, pp. 105–107)

5.   *For the creation was subjected to frustration, not by its own choice, but by the will of the one who subjected it, in hope ²¹that the creation itself will be liberated from its bondage to decay and brought into the glorious freedom of the children of God.* Romans 8:20–21 (NIV)

To what does the word creation refer in this passage? What is the promise given in verse 21? (*Heaven*, pp. 126–129)

6.   Compare life on our present earth with life as it will be on the New Earth based upon Isaiah 65:17–25. How does this description give us hope?

"Behold, I will create new heavens and a new earth. The former things will not be remembered, nor will they come to mind. ¹⁸But be glad and rejoice forever in what I will create, for I will create Jerusalem to be a delight and its people a joy. ¹⁹I will rejoice over Jerusalem and take delight in my people; the sound of weeping and of crying will be heard in it no more.

²⁰Never again will there be in it an infant who lives but a few days, or an old man who does not live out his years; he who dies at a hundred will be thought a mere youth; he who fails to reach a hundred will be considered accursed. ²¹They will build houses and dwell in them; they will plant vineyards and eat their fruit. ²²No longer will they build houses and others live in them, or plant and others eat. For as the days of a tree, so will be the days of my people; my chosen ones will long enjoy the works of their hands. ²³They will not toil in vain or bear children doomed to misfortune; for they will be a people blessed by the LORD, they and their descendants with them. ²⁴Before they call I will answer; while they are still speaking I will hear. ²⁵The wolf and the lamb will feed together, and the lion will eat straw like the ox, but dust will be the serpent's food. They will neither harm nor destroy on all my holy mountain," says the LORD. Isaiah 65:17–25 (NIV)

In the video teaching, Randy Alcorn said that there are many characteristics of this earth that we can look to as reference points as we envision the New Earth. Discuss which of the earth's present characteristics you look forward to seeing in the New Earth in their un-fallen state. (*Heaven*, pp. 15–18, 241–247)

7. *I now establish my covenant with you and with your descendants after you* [10] *and with every living creature that was with you—the birds, the livestock and all the wild animals, all those that came out of the ark with you—every living creature on earth.* Genesis 9:9–10 (NIV)

    According to Genesis 9:9, with whom does God establish his covenant? What does this suggest about how God feels about animals and their likely inclusion on the New Earth?

8. Luke 22:30 says, *...you may eat and drink at my table in my kingdom...* (NIV). We *will* eat and drink at the Lord's table in Heaven. Discuss what you think it will be like to dine with the King of kings. (*Heaven*, pp. 301–309)

9. Randy Alcorn said, "We will be learning through eternity about the meaning of God's grace in our lives." First Corinthians 13:12 says, *Now we see things imperfectly as in a poor mirror, but then we will see everything with perfect clarity. All that I know now is partial and incomplete, but then I will know everything completely, just as God knows me now* (NLT). How does it feel to know that we'll someday be able to grasp the full measure of God's grace? (*Heaven*, pp. 318–319)

10. Job was certain that death was not the end of his existence and that once he died he would stand before God in his own flesh and see him with his own eyes. In Job 19:26–27 he says, *And after my skin has been destroyed, yet in my flesh I will see God; ²⁷I myself will see him with my own eyes—I, and not another. How my heart yearns within me!* (NIV). What does Job's declaration say about meeting our Redeemer?

 SHARING YOUR LIFE MISSION EVERY DAY (10 MIN)

Death is not the end of our existence. Of this we can be certain. We can be equally certain that when we die we will see our Savior face-to-face. This assurance provides believers with hope, and allows us to persevere in even the most difficult circumstances because we know this life is not all there is. 1 Peter 3:15 tells us to *always be prepared to give an answer to everyone who asks you to give the reason for the hope that you have* (NIV). Have you prepared yourself to share your hope in Christ with others?

11. During our previous weeks, you've given prayerful consideration to others you know who need to meet Jesus Christ. It is through personal relationship with Jesus that they too can have assurance of their redemption. Commit this week to share with one person on your *Circles of Life* diagram from session one.

12. In your *Personal Health Plan* on page 111, next to the "Sharing" icon, answer the "WHEN are you shepherding another person in Christ?" question. If you aren't currently shepherding someone in their faith, think about how your spiritual partner might help prepare you for this.

PRAYER AND SURRENDER (10 MIN)

13. As you wrap up your time today, pray that the Lord would open your heart and mind to the ideas presented in this session. Ask him for clarity on issues that seem confusing. Thank him for the wonderful creation that is to come on the New Earth.

14. Share prayer requests in your group and record the requests and praises on the *Prayer and Praise Report* beginning on page 123. Commit to praying for each other throughout the week between group meetings.

15. It is important for all believers to draw near to God for a few minutes each day. Continue using the *Reflections* at the end of each session to help you focus on the principles of this study and spend time with God.

Note: We suggest you read *Days 29* through *35* in the *50 Days of Heaven* book as you work through the *Reflections*. If you don't have time to work through all the *Reflections* before your next group meeting, we suggest you work through the day(s) marked with an asterisk.

SCRIPTURE STUDY

If you want to dig deeper into what the Bible says about the topic at hand, we've provided suggested study passages below. The *Growing* section provides you with plenty to discuss within the group, so we recommend that participants study these passages on their own between group meetings, if desired.

- 1 Corinthians 6:20; 10:31
- 1 Peter 1:12
- 2 Peter 3:5–7
- 1 Timothy 6:17
- Ephesians 2:6–7
- Exodus 28–29
- Ezekiel 36:35
- Genesis 1:25, 30; 2:7; 6:17, 19–20; 7:15, 22; 9:9–17
- Isaiah 11:6–9; 25:6; 35:1; 51:3; 55:13; 62:2; 65:15, 17, 25; 66:22
- Job 19:26–27
- John 20:28; 21:4–14
- Luke 9:17, 19; 15:4–7, 10; 14:12–24; 16:25; 19:17, 19; 22:18, 29–30; 24:39
- Matthew 7:9–11; 8:11; 16:25; 26:28
- Philippians 3:20–21
- Revelation 2:7, 17; 3:12; 8:21–23; 19:9; 20:15, 21:4, 10–11, 15–16, 18–19, 21, 27; 22:1–2

REFLECTIONS

Each day, read a *Reflection* below, giving prayerful consideration to what you learn about God, his Spirit, and his place in your life. If you don't have time to work through all the *Reflections* before your next group meeting, we suggest you work through the day(s) marked with an asterisk.

*Day 29 – The New Earth: A Greater Eden

In order to get a glimpse into the New Earth, we must take a close look at the present earth. The people around us, the earth's natural wonders and the joys of life are all but shadows of what the earth once was and foretastes of what it yet will be when it is renewed. On the New Earth, we will see this present earth in its un-fallen state, full of all the good things of God's natural creation enhanced into something far greater than we've ever seen or experienced before.

> *Indeed, the LORD will comfort Zion; He will comfort all her waste places. And her wilderness he will make like Eden, and her desert like the garden of the LORD; joy and gladness will be found in her, thanksgiving and sound of a melody.* Isaiah 51:3 (NASB)

Reflection: What are some of the good things from God's natural creation or from your own life that you'd like to see God carry over to the New Earth?

_____

_____

_____

_____

_____

_____

Day 30 – Animals on the New Earth?

Scripture suggests that people and animals are both unique living beings, created by God and included in the everlasting covenant promise.

> *So God said to Noah, "This is the sign of the covenant I have established between me and all life on the earth."* Genesis 9:17 (NIV)

Reflection: Consider God's creative work in animals. Why do you think he counted them important enough to include in his covenant promise?

_____

_____

_____

_____

_____

_____

_____

_____

_____

_____

_____

_____

_____

_____

_____

Day 31 – Animals We Love Might Live Again

While animals are not said to have eternal souls, God is their maker and he promises to make "all things new" (Revelation 21:5). He also says the "whole creation" is groaning awaiting redemption. Since there is biblical reason to believe animals will be on the New Earth, couldn't God easily recreate our beloved pets to be among them?

> *We know that the whole creation has been groaning as in the pains of childbirth right up to the present time.* [23]*Not only so, but we ourselves, who have the firstfruits of the Spirit, groan inwardly as we wait eagerly for our adoption as sons, the redemption of our bodies.* Romans 8:22–23 (NIV)

Reflection: How has God used a pet in your life? What attributes of God are you reminded of?

_____

_____

_____

_____

_____

_____

_____

_____

_____

_____

_____

_____

*Day 32 – The New Jerusalem

The Bible describes the magnificence of the New Jerusalem in great detail saying, *It shone with the glory of God, and its brilliance was like that of a very precious jewel, like a jasper, clear as crystal.* Revelation 21:10–11 (NIV). Amid the glorious architecture and beautiful natural wonders on the New Earth, we'll have everything we need for strength, vitality and excitement for life. Best of all, no matter where we go or what we do, we'll never leave the presence of the King.

> *No longer will there be any curse. The throne of God and of the Lamb will be in the city, and his servants will serve him. ⁴They will see his face, and his name will be on their foreheads.* Revelation 22:3–4 (NIV)

Reflection: What about life in the Great City appeals to you most? Is there anything you are thankful won't be part of life in the New Jerusalem?

_____

_____

_____

_____

_____

_____

_____

_____

_____

_____

_____

_____

*Day 33 – Being Ourselves in Heaven

A central part of our bodily resurrection will be the continuity of our identity. We will be ourselves in Heaven. We will become like Jesus in character, yet remain the distinct individuals he delighted in creating.

> *"As surely as my new heavens and earth will remain, so will you always be my people, with a name that will never disappear," says the LORD.* Isaiah 66:22 (NLT)

Reflection: How can you begin your transformation into the person that God created you to be this side of Heaven?

_____

_____

_____

_____

_____

_____

_____

_____

_____

_____

_____

_____

_____

_____

_____

Day 34 – Eating and Drinking on the New Earth

Scripture is packed with references to eating, drinking, and feasting in Heaven. God made us to enjoy food and to enjoy celebrating with one another. The same God who delights in our pleasures will be glorified in our grateful praise.

> *So whether you eat or drink or whatever you do, do it all for the glory of God.*
> 1 Corinthians 10:31 (NIV)

Reflection: God wants us to look forward to eating at his table in his kingdom. Imagine and describe what it might be like to share a meal or a cup of coffee or tea with your Savior.

_____

_____

_____

_____

_____

_____

_____

_____

_____

_____

_____

_____

Day 35 – Knowing and Learning

God alone is omniscient. When we join our Lord in Heaven, we will gain clarity and understanding but we will remain finite, limited beings. We will not experience sudden and complete knowledge but a gradual, progressive and ongoing revelation of God's grace.

Now we see but a poor reflection as in a mirror; then we shall see face to face. Now I know in part; then I shall know fully, even as I am fully known. 1 Corinthians 13:12 (NIV)

Reflection: What do you wish you knew now that you anticipate learning in Heaven?

_____

_____

_____

_____

_____

_____

_____

_____

_____

_____

_____

_____

_____

SESSION 6: RELATIONSHIPS IN HEAVEN

Memory Verse: *Brothers, we do not want you to be ignorant about those who fall asleep, or to grieve like the rest of men, who have no hope...we who are still alive and are left will be caught up together with them in the clouds to meet the Lord in the air. And so we will be with the Lord forever.* 1 Thessalonians 4:13, 17 (NIV)

Most people think about Heaven at least some time in their life. We might wonder what our relationships will be like, whether we will see and recognize each other when we get there, or we contemplate whether we will remember what happened to us during our lives on earth.

Missionary Amy Carmichael wrote in answer to these questions... "Shall we know one another in Heaven? Shall we love and remember? I do not think anyone need wonder about this or doubt for a single moment. We are never told we shall, because, I expect, it was not necessary to say anything about this which our own hearts tell us. We do not need words. For if we think for a minute, we know. Would you be yourself if you did not love and remember?

We are told that we shall be like our Lord Jesus. Surely this does not mean in holiness only, but in everything; and does not he know and love and remember? He would not be himself if he did not, and we should not be ourselves if we did not."[1]

Open your group with prayer.

 CONNECTING WITH GOD'S FAMILY (10 MIN)

Being certain that we will see our loved ones again in eternity, and that we will know and remember all that is familiar to us, is a great comfort. In this session we will explore these thoughts further.

---

[1] Randy Alcorn, *Heaven*, Tyndale House Publishers, Inc., 2004, p 346–347, quoted from Amy Carmichael, *Thou Givest ...They Gather*, quoted in *Images of Heaven: Reflections on Glory*, comp. Lil Copan and Anna Trimiew (Wheaton, IL: Harold Shaw, 1996), 111.

1. Share one thing about your most treasured relationships (spouse, children, friends) that you would like to see continue in Heaven.

Watch the DVD teaching for this session now. After watching the video, have someone read the discussion questions in the *Growing* section and direct the group discussion.

GROWING TO BE LIKE CHRIST (45 MIN)

In First Thessalonians chapter four, Paul spoke of what we can expect regarding our loved ones after their physical bodies die here on earth. Because of Christ's resurrection we have assurance that our loved ones are not lost to us. We will be reunited with them, we will know them, and we will have continuity from this life in Heaven. Remembering is an aspect of our humanity that we can count on when we leave earth as it is today.

2. Often we refer to the death of a loved one as our "loss." What perspective does 1 Thessalonians 4:13 and 17 give us about this?

   Brothers, we do not want you to be ignorant about those who fall asleep, or to grieve like the rest of men, who have no hope...we who are still alive and are left will be caught up together with them in the clouds to meet the Lord in the air. And so we will be with the Lord forever. 1 Thessalonians 4:13, 17 (NIV)

   How can the fact that we will be reunited with believers in Heaven affect our grief over our loved ones' deaths? (*Heaven*, pp. 342–343)

3. How might Emily's story help us encourage someone who has a terminal illness? (*Heaven*, p. 462)

4. In Matthew 22:30, Jesus described to the religious leaders what the marriage relationship will look like at the resurrection.

    At the resurrection people will neither marry nor be given in marriage; they will be like the angels in heaven. Matthew 22:30 (NIV)

    Psalm 103:20–21 gives us a great picture of what the angels in Heaven are like. *Bless the Lord, you his angels, Mighty in strength, who perform his word, Obeying the voice of his word! ²¹Bless the Lord, all you his hosts, You who serve him, doing his will.* (NASB)

    What does this say to you about our relationships and purpose for life in Heaven?

5. Revelation 19:5–8 speaks of the marriage of the Lamb.

    Then a voice came from the throne, saying: "Praise our God, all you his servants, you who fear him, both small and great!" ⁶Then I heard what sounded like a great multitude, like the roar of rushing waters and like loud peals of thunder, shouting: "Hallelujah! For our Lord God Almighty reigns. ⁷Let us rejoice and be glad and give him glory! For the wedding of the <u>Lamb</u> has come, and his <u>bride</u> has made herself ready. ⁸Fine linen, bright and clean, was given her to wear." (Fine linen stands for the righteous acts of the saints.) Revelation 19:5–8 (NIV)

    Who do you understand the Lamb and his bride to be? How did Randy's explanation of the marriage relationship between Jesus and his bride promise to satisfy our need for intimate relationships? (*Heaven*, pp. 350–351)

6. *"Do not let your hearts be troubled. Trust in God; trust also in me. ²In my Father's house are many rooms; if it were not so, I would have told you. I am going there to prepare a place for you. ³And if I go and prepare a place for you, I will come back and take you to be with me that you also may be where I am. ⁴You know the way to the place where I am going."* John 14:1–4 (NIV)

   With John 14:1–4 in mind, what do you imagine your present and future relationships will be like in Heaven?

7. In his teaching today, Randy talked about how we will remember our lives on earth when we get to Heaven. Remembering without pain and suffering will allow us to have God's perspective of the circumstances we lived through here on earth. Talk about how God's perspective might be different from our own. How do you think this new understanding might bless us? (*Heaven*, pp. 343–344)

8. Heaven will be a melting pot of ethnic and national diversity and people will be united in their worship of King Jesus. We will delight in our differences without resentment and fear. Discuss how you think this should affect the way we live our lives on this earth. (*Heaven*, pp. 376–377)

9. *Blessed are you who hunger now, for you will be satisfied. Blessed are you who weep now, for you will laugh. ²³Rejoice in that day and leap for joy, because great is your reward in heaven.* Luke 6:21, 23a (NIV)

   God redeems our lost opportunities—especially those lost through our faithful service. The New Earth will be a second chance to do things we missed out on. How does this help you understand what the world to come will be like? (*Heaven*, pp. 371–373)

10. In what ways has this study challenged you or given you comfort? Is there an area where you need to trust God more? How can your small group help you do this?

 PRAYER AND SURRENDER (25 MIN)

Even though most of us likely believe that Heaven will be a wonderful place, some of us may be struggling with questions that still feel like unknowns.

11. Pair up with your spiritual partner now and look back at your *Spiritual Health Assessment* from session two. Take a few minutes to re-evaluate your responses in the *Prayer and Surrender* section. Share with your partner one area you feel you have grown in and one area that still needs some work.

    Turn to the *Personal Health Plan* on page 111 and individually consider the "HOW are you surrendering your heart?" question.

12. Our next session is the last in this study on Heaven. In the *Prayer and Surrender* section of session seven, you will be encouraged to share the *Lord's Supper* or a *Foot-washing* together, or participate in a *Surrendering at the Cross* exercise. Read the instructions for each of these now, and talk about what your group would like to do. The instructions can be found in the *Appendix* beginning on page 114.

13. As a group spend some time in prayer praising God for restored relationships in Heaven. Thank him that eternity has plenty of time for you to enjoy again the people who influenced you for God's glory while you lived on earth. And thank him for the opportunity to continue to meet new friends and develop relationships in Heaven.

Share prayer requests in your group and record the requests and praises on the *Prayer and Praise Report* on page 123. Commit to praying for each other throughout the week between group meetings.

14. It is important for all believers to draw near to God for a few minutes each day. Continue using the *Reflections* at the end of each session to help you focus on the principles of this study as well as spending time with God.

Note: We suggest you read *Days 36* through *42* in the *50 Days of Heaven* book as you work through the *Reflections*. If you don't have time to work through all the *Reflections* before your next group meeting, we suggest you work through the day(s) marked with an asterisk.

SCRIPTURE STUDY

If you want to dig deeper into the Bible passages about the topic at hand, we've provided suggested study passages below. The *Growing* section provides you with plenty to discuss within the group, so we recommend that participants study these passages on their own between group meetings, if desired.

- 1 Corinthians 15:6
- 1 Thessalonians 3:6, 9–10; 4:13–18
- Acts 17:26
- Ephesians 2:14–16, 19; 5:31–32
- Genesis 1:28; 2:15, 18; 3:17–19; 4:20–22; 9:1, 20
- Isaiah 65:17
- Jeremiah 31:34
- John 4:34; 5:17; 20:24–29; 21
- Luke 2:14; 6:2, 21; 8:19–21; 9:29–33; 16:4, 9
- Mark 10:29–30
- Matthew 22:30; 25:23
- Revelation 5:9–10, 14:13; 21:12–14, 24–26; 22:3
- Romans 8:18

REFLECTIONS

Each day, read a *Reflection* below, giving prayerful consideration to what you learn about God, his Spirit, and his place in your life. If you don't have time to work through all the *Reflections* before your next group meeting, we suggest you work through the day(s) marked with an asterisk.

Day 36 – Resting and Working

Although we will experience rest from our labor, we will have the energy and passion for doing the kind of work in Heaven that will energize and fulfill us. This work will bring us significance and joy. We'll be grateful for the opportunity to bring unending glory to God.

> *Then I heard a voice from heaven say, "Write: Blessed are the dead who die in the Lord from now on." "Yes," says the Spirit, "they will rest from their labor, for their deeds will follow them."* Revelation 14:13 (NIV)

Reflection: How can you begin to glorify God in everything you do today? What can you do to begin to understand his perspective in every circumstance in which you find yourself?

_____

_____

_____

_____

_____

_____

_____

*Day 37 – Remembering and Recognizing

We have every reason to look forward to recognizing and remembering our family and friends in Heaven. We'll rejoice in God's presence for the things we experienced together, both good and bad, because we'll view them through God's perspective. We will see and understand his purposes for everything that happened while we walked on this earth.

> *Brothers, we do not want you to be ignorant about those who fall asleep, or to grieve like the rest of men, who have no hope...we who are still alive and are left will be caught up together with them in the clouds to meet the Lord in the air. And so we will be with the Lord forever.* 1 Thessalonians 4:13, 17 (NIV)

Reflection: Write out your praises to God for his plans and purposes for your time here on earth. Ask him to open your eyes to see his goodness and love in the midst of trials and struggles. How can you begin to let his love for you surpass every loss, confusion, and grief you experience on this earth?

_____

_____

_____

_____

_____

_____

_____

_____

_____

_____

Day 38 – Marriage and Family

The Bible teaches that there will be only one marriage in Heaven, the marriage between Christ and his bride, the Church. All believers in Christ will be included as his bride. God's ideal for marriage will finally be realized and we'll enjoy fully satisfying relationships.

> *...for we are members of his body.* [31]*"For this reason a man will leave his father and mother and be united to his wife, and the two will become one flesh."* [32]*This is a profound mystery—but I am talking about Christ and the church.* Ephesians 5:31–32 (NIV)

Reflection: How can you begin to glorify God daily in your family relationships?

_____

_____

_____

_____

_____

_____

_____

_____

_____

_____

_____

_____

Day 39 – Friendships in Heaven: Old and New

Most people have some close friends; some people have only one very close friend with several acquaintances. Others have several friends they consider close to them and many they call acquaintances. These relationships are not accidents and don't happen by chance. God has chosen the timing and circumstances of all our relationships, both here and in eternity.

From one man he made every nation of men—that they should inhabit the whole earth; and he determined the times set for them and the exact places where they should live. Acts 17:26 (NIV)

Reflection: God created us to need other people and one day all our friendships will rise to their highest levels, nourished in God's presence. How do you feel about meeting new people and developing new friendships in Heaven? What sounds exciting about the idea?

_____

_____

_____

_____

_____

_____

_____

_____

_____

_____

_____

_____

Day 40 – Lost Opportunities Regained

Jesus promised that though we weep now through our sufferings, we will be rewarded in Heaven. And he has promised that he is working all things for our good now (Romans 8:28). But we may also feel a sense of loss when remembering missed opportunities and we can have confidence that in Heaven we will be comforted, fulfilled and rewarded. Missed opportunities will be new opportunities when the curse is lifted and death is forever reversed.

> *Blessed are you who hunger now, for you will be satisfied. Blessed are you who weep now, for you will laugh. ... [23]Rejoice in that day and leap for joy, because great is your reward in heaven...* Luke 6:21, 23 (NIV)

Reflection: What lost opportunities would you like God to restore on the New Earth? Who do you know that you would like to see God reward for their faithfulness by restoring their lost opportunities? How do God's character and his promises in the Bible give you confidence that he will do this?

_____

_____

_____

_____

_____

_____

_____

_____

_____

_____

_____

Day 41 – Races and Nations

Like the current Jerusalem, the New Jerusalem will have a diverse mix of ethnic groups and nationalities. But unlike the current city, the groups in the New Jerusalem will be united by their common worship of King Jesus. They will delight in each other's differences, and never resent them or be frightened by them.

> *And they sang a new song with these words: "You are worthy ...For you were slaughtered, and your blood has ransomed people for God from every tribe and language and people and nation. [10] And you have caused them to become a Kingdom of priests for our God. And they will reign on the earth...."* Revelation 5:9–10 (NIV)

Reflection: How do you think God will be glorified in Heaven by our differences? What can people do today to glorify God through, and/or in spite of, our differences?

_____

_____

_____

_____

_____

_____

_____

_____

_____

_____

_____

Day 42 – The Development of Culture

Things like art, music, literature, crafts, technology, clothing, jewelry, education, food preparation—all are part of society or culture, the creative accomplishments of God's image-bearers. Way back in Genesis 2 we begin to see culture taking shape. Revelation 21:24 and 26 give the biblical basis to believe that the best culture, history, art, music, and languages of the old earth will be redeemed, purified, and carried over to the New Earth.

> *The nations will walk by its light, and the kings of the earth will bring their splendor into it [the New Jerusalem]* [26] *The glory and honor of the nations will be brought into it.* Revelation 21:24, 26 (NIV)

Reflection: What do you look forward to seeing in the culture on the New Earth? How do you think this will glorify God in eternity?

_____

_____

_____

_____

_____

_____

_____

_____

_____

_____

_____

_____

SESSION 7: OUR GREATEST ADVENTURE

Memory Verse: *...In Your presence is fullness of joy; At Your right hand are pleasures forevermore.* Psalm 16:11 (NKJV)

While we can expect to experience disappointments in this life, the life that awaits us in Heaven is filled with excitement, adventure, and fulfilled dreams. One misconception about Heaven is that it will be boring. The truth is that our imaginative and exciting God created the beauty, splendor, and majesty in the world for us to explore and enjoy. Everything that we currently love about this creation will be renewed again on the New Earth. Not only that, but God also created us with the capacity to do the very things that he set in our hearts to dream. Certainly, we will not find ourselves bored!

Open your group with prayer.

CONNECTING WITH GOD'S FAMILY (10 MIN)

A New Heaven and a New Earth await us. In this session, we'll take a closer look at what God has for us to do in Heaven and how his plan reflects his love for us.

1. Share with the group how your thoughts about Heaven have been challenged during this study. Is there something that you learned that has caused a heightened anticipation for Heaven?

2. If your group still needs to make decisions about continuing to meet after this session, have that discussion now. Talk about what you will study, who will lead, and where and when you will meet.

    Review the *Group Values* on page 7 and evaluate how well you met your goals. Discuss any changes you want to make as you move forward. As your group starts a new study this is a great time to take on a new role or change roles of service in your group. What new role will you take on? If you are uncertain, maybe your group members have some ideas for you. Remember you aren't making a lifetime commitment to the new role; it will only be for a few weeks. Maybe someone would like to share a role with you if you don't feel ready to serve solo.

Watch the DVD teaching for this session now. After watching the video, have someone read the discussion questions in the *Growing* section and direct the group discussion.

 GROWING TO BE LIKE CHRIST (50 MIN)

We have eternity to spend in Heaven with God. Contrary to what some may think, every experience in Heaven will be more exciting and more fulfilling than any experience we've had here on this earth. Our lives will be abundant, full of adventure, revelation, and joy.

3. Jesus instructed his disciples in Luke 6:23 to: *Rejoice in that day and leap for joy, because great is your reward in heaven. For that is how their fathers treated the prophets* (NIV).

    What reward do you think Jesus is referring to? How does this particular promise give us reason to rejoice?

4. *You have made known to me the path of life; you will fill me with joy in your presence, with eternal pleasures at your right hand.* Psalm 16:11 (NIV)

    According to this verse, what will we experience in God's presence? (*Heaven*, pp. 409–411)

5. In the video teaching, Randy Alcorn said we will forever see God's wonder and glory as we explore the New Heavens and the

New Earth. Read the verses that follow. Aside from exploring the new creation, what will occupy our time in Heaven?

Then I heard every creature in heaven and on earth and under the earth and on the sea, and all that is in them, singing: "To him who sits on the throne and to the Lamb be praise and honor and glory and power, for ever and ever!" Revelation 5:13 (NIV)

Therefore, "they are before the throne of God and serve him day and night in his temple; and he who sits on the throne will spread his tent over them." Revelation 7:15 (NIV)

There will be no more night. They will not need the light of a lamp or the light of the sun, for the Lord God will give them light. And they will reign for ever and ever. Revelation 22:5 (NIV)

6. John 14:1–3 says, *Let not your heart be troubled; believe in God, believe also in Me. ²In My Father's house are many dwelling places; if it were not so, I would have told you; for I go to prepare a place for you. ³And if I go and prepare a place for you, I will come again, and receive you to Myself; that where I am, there you may be also* (NASB).

    Why should we not allow our hearts to be troubled according to these verses? Discuss how this promise relates to unfulfilled dreams or desires. (*Heaven*, pp. 431–436)

7. What reasons does Colossians 3:1–4 give for why we should be focused on Heaven? (*Heaven*, pp. 201–203)

    Since you have been raised to new life with Christ, set your sights on the realities of heaven, where Christ sits at God's right hand in the place of honor and power. ²Let heaven fill your thoughts. Do not think only about things down here on earth. ³For you died when Christ died, and your real life is hidden with Christ in God. ⁴And when Christ, who is your real life, is revealed to the whole world, you will share in all his glory. Colossians 3:1–4 (NLT)

8. Randy Alcorn said, "We can be genuinely excited about Heaven...that is part of being genuinely excited about God because Heaven is God's home that he is preparing for us." Please read Ecclesiastes 3:11 below.

He has made everything beautiful in its time. He has also set eternity in the hearts of men; yet they cannot fathom what God has done from beginning to end. Ecclesiastes 3:11 (NIV)

What is set in the hearts of men? Who set it there and what does this suggest to you about the appropriateness of our longing for Heaven? (*Heaven*, p. 114)

9. Take turns reading the verses that follow.

Fix your thoughts on what is true and honorable and right. Think about things that are pure and lovely and admirable. Think about things that are excellent and worthy of praise. ⁹Keep putting into practice all you learned from me and heard from me and saw me doing, and the God of peace will be with you. Philippians 4:8b–9 (NLT)

Since God chose you to be the holy people whom he loves, you must clothe yourselves with tenderhearted mercy, kindness, humility, gentleness, and patience. ¹³You must make allowance for each other's faults and forgive the person who offends you. Remember, the Lord forgave you, so you must forgive others. ¹⁴And the most important piece of clothing you must wear is love. Love is what binds us all together in perfect harmony. ¹⁵And let the peace that comes from Christ rule in your hearts. For as members of one body you are all called to live in peace. And always be thankful. Colossians 3:12–15 (NLT)

Letting Heaven fill our thoughts means putting Heaven's priorities into daily practice as we focus on eternity. How can we do this according to Philippians 4:8–9 and Colossians 3:12–15? (*Heaven*, pp. 470–472)

10. In closing this study Randy Alcorn said, "Our adventures don't end in this life. The greatest adventures are ahead of us. The best is yet to come." What long awaited adventure do you anticipate experiencing in Heaven?

 PRAYER AND SURRENDER (10 MIN)

Filling our thoughts with Heaven requires that we first realize that our real life *is* Christ and surrender ourselves to him.

11. Spend a few minutes reflecting on your own life. Is Christ your life, or is he just a part of it? Ask God to reveal to you any area(s) that you may be holding back and surrender them to him now.

12. Take time now to share the *Lord's Supper*, a *Foot-washing*, or the *Surrendering at the Cross* exercise. Begin by praying for God's presence and direction in this activity. Instructions for these activities are found beginning on page 114 in the *Appendix*.

13. As you wrap up this final session of the Heaven study, pray that the Lord would bring clarity to your mind and peace to your heart on issues that you may still have questions.

    Thank God for the revelation that he has given you during these seven sessions about his wonderful new creation that is to come. Give him praise for new or deepened relationships within your small group.

    You may want to spend a few minutes looking back over the *Prayer and Praise Reports* and give thanks for answered prayer.

Note: We suggest you read *Days 42* through *50* in the *50 Days of Heaven* book as you work through the *Reflections*. If you don't have time to work through all the *Reflections* before your next group meeting, we suggest you work through the day(s) marked with an asterisk.

SCRIPTURE STUDY

If you want to dig deeper into the Bible passages about the topic at hand, we've provided suggested study passages below. The *Growing* section provides you with plenty to discuss within the group, so we recommend that participants study these passages on their own between group meetings, if desired.

- 1 John 3:3
- Ephesians 2:10
- Hebrews 11:16; 12:28
- John 14:23
- Luke 6:20–23, 24; 16:10–12; 19:11–27
- Matthew 5:3–5; 6:20
- Philippians 1:23, 3:13–14
- Proverbs 4:18
- Psalm 16:11
- Revelation 21:1, 3–5; 7:15; 13:6; 22:3

REFLECTIONS

Each day, read a *Reflection* below, giving prayerful consideration to what you learn about God, his Spirit, and his place in your life. If you don't have time to work through all the *Reflections* before your next group meeting, we suggest you work through those marked with an asterisk.

Day 43 – Laughter

God made us to laugh and to love to laugh. Our theology must include humor if we are to be prepared for an eternity full of celebration, spontaneous laughter, and overflowing joy. When we see God in Heaven, he won't only wipe away our tears, he'll fill our hearts with joy and our mouths with laughter.

> *God blesses you who are hungry now, for you will be satisfied. God blesses you who weep now, for the time will come when you will laugh with joy.* Luke 6:21 (NLT)

Reflection: How are you experiencing the joy of Christ so that your life is full of laughter now? Are you looking forward to laughing in Heaven?

_____

_____

_____

_____

_____

_____

_____

*Day 44 – No More Boredom

Satan would have us believe that sin is exciting but righteousness is boring. On the contrary, freedom from sin is what allows us to be who God intended and to find far greater joy in everything. Once in Heaven, we'll experience even greater joys than we knew on earth. We will work, play, and serve God while we reign with him for eternity—this will certainly not be boring.

> *You will show me the path of life; In your presence is fullness of joy; At your right hand are pleasures forevermore.* Psalm 16:11 (NKJV)

Reflection: Of all the exciting things we'll do in Heaven that bring God glory, what are some you look forward to most?

_____

_____

_____

_____

_____

_____

_____

_____

_____

_____

_____

_____

*Day 45 – Dreams Fulfilled

This is not our only chance at life on earth. God's promise to us is not only to remove the heartbreaks of this earth, but to make up for them. In Heaven, we will experience the fulfillment of our God-given dreams and desires that went unrealized on earth.

> *He fulfills the desires of those who fear him; he hears their cry and saves them.*
> Psalm 145:19 (NIV)

Reflection: What unfulfilled God-given dreams or desires do you want to see fulfilled in Heaven?

_____

_____

_____

_____

_____

_____

_____

_____

_____

_____

_____

_____

_____

*Day 46 – New Opportunities on the New Earth

When you experience disappointment and loss as you faithfully serve God, remember that the loss is temporary but the gains will be eternal. The better we use our time and opportunities for God's glory here, the greater our opportunities will be in Heaven. When it comes time for us to leave this earth, we may lose out on some opportunities, but every day spent on the New Earth will be a new opportunity to live out the dreams that matter most.

> *Whoever can be trusted with very little can also be trusted with much...* Luke 16:10 (NIV)

Reflection: How are you spending your life faithfully serving God while on this earth? What opportunities on the New Earth excite you?

_____

_____

_____

_____

_____

_____

_____

_____

_____

_____

_____

_____

*Day 47 – Plus Ultra: More Beyond

Sadly, many Christians store up most of their treasures on earth so that every day they move closer to death, they move farther from their treasures. We should store up our treasures in Heaven so the closer we are to death the closer we are to our treasures. As we spend our lives heading toward our treasures by making daily choices to honor God, we will have reason to rejoice.

> *But store up for yourselves treasures in Heaven, where moth and rust do not destroy, and where thieves do not break in and steal.* [21]*For where your treasure is, there your heart will be also.* Matthew 6:20–21 (NIV)

Reflection: What choices are you making today that put your treasures in Heaven?

_____

_____

_____

_____

_____

_____

_____

_____

_____

_____

_____

_____

*Day 48 – No Rivalry Between Christ and Heaven

Every thought of Heaven should move our hearts toward God, just as every thought of God will move our hearts toward Heaven. Heaven is not an idol that competes with God; it is a lens by which we see God more clearly. If Heaven fills our hearts and minds, God will fill our hearts and minds.

> *Instead, they were longing for a better country—a heavenly one. Therefore God is not ashamed to be called their God, for he has prepared a city for them.* Hebrews 11:16 (NIV)

Reflection: What do you anticipate most about Heaven and how do you think it will help to move your heart toward God?

_____

_____

_____

_____

_____

_____

_____

_____

_____

_____

_____

_____

_____

Day 49 – Reepicheep and Emily

Each of us will someday die. Since the majority of our lives will be spent on the other side of death, we must be careful in this life to prepare for what awaits us there. We should be so excited about what's on the other side of death's door that we live our life as a great adventure with one destination in mind: Heaven.

> *Since, then, you have been raised with Christ, set your hearts on things above, where Christ is seated at the right hand of God. ²Set your minds on things above, not on earthly things.* Colossians 3:1–2 (NIV)

Reflection: What are some things you can do to increase your anticipation of Heaven, to live in light of eternity?

_____

_____

_____

_____

_____

_____

_____

_____

_____

_____

_____

_____

Day 50 – It Doesn't Get Any Better Than This ... Or Does It?

Thinking of Heaven inevitably leads to pursuing holiness. It's when our minds drift from Jesus and Heaven, that sin seems attractive. Thinking of Heaven and the New Earth will motivate us to live each day in profound thankfulness to God and lead us to an eternity with the Lord we love and the family and friends we cherish. Our experiences on the New Earth will be far better than the best we have experienced on this earth.

> *And everyone who has this hope fixed on him purifies himself, just as he is pure.*
> 1 John 3:3 (NASB)

Reflection: Whom could you comfort today with the thought that those who love Jesus will someday experience God's best?

_____

_____

_____

_____

_____

_____

_____

_____

_____

_____

_____

_____

FREQUENTLY ASKED QUESTIONS

What do we do on the first night of our group?

Like all fun things in life–have a party! A "get to know you" coffee, dinner, or dessert is a great way to launch a new study. You may want to review the *Group Values* (page 7) and share the names of a few friends you can invite to join you. But most importantly, have fun before your study time begins.

Where do we find new members for our group?

This can be troubling, especially for new groups that have only a few people or for existing groups that lose a few people along the way. We encourage you to pray with your group and then brainstorm a list of people from work, church, your neighborhood, your children's school, family, the gym, and so forth. Then have each group member invite several of the people on his or her list. Another good strategy is to ask church leaders to make an announcement or allow a bulletin insert.

No matter how you find members, it's vital that you stay on the lookout for new people to join your group. All groups tend to go through healthy attrition—the result of moves, releasing new leaders, ministry opportunities, and so forth—and if the group gets too small, it could be at risk of shutting down. If you and your group stay open, you'll be amazed at the people God sends your way. The next person just might become a friend for life. You never know!

How long will this group meet?

It's totally up to the group—once you come to the end of this study. Most groups meet weekly for at least their first several weeks, but every other week can work as well. We strongly recommend that the group meet for the first six months on a weekly basis if at all possible. This allows for continuity, and if people miss a meeting they aren't gone for a whole month.

At the end of this study, each group member may decide if he or she wants to continue on for another study. Some groups launch relationships for years to come, and others are stepping-stones into another group experience. Either way, enjoy the journey.

What if this group is not working for me?

You're not alone! This could be the result of a personality conflict, life stage difference, geographical distance, level of spiritual maturity, or any number of things. Relax. Pray for God's direction, and at the end of this seven-week study, decide whether to continue with this group or find another. You don't buy the first car you look at or marry the first person you date, and the same goes with a group. Don't bail out before the seven weeks are up—God might have something to teach you. Also, don't run from conflict or prejudge people before you have given them a chance. God is still working in you too!

Who is the leader?

Most groups have an official leader. But ideally, the group will mature and members will rotate the leadership of meetings. We have discovered that healthy groups rotate hosts/leaders and homes on a regular basis. This model ensures that all members grow, give their unique contribution, and develop their gifts. This study guide and the Holy Spirit can keep things on track even when you rotate leaders. Christ has promised to be in your midst as you gather. Ultimately, God is your leader each step of the way.

How do we handle the child care needs in our group?

Very carefully. Seriously, this can be a sensitive issue. We suggest that you empower the group to openly brainstorm solutions. You may try one option that works for a while and then adjust over time. Our favorite approach is for adults to meet in the living room or dining room, and to share the cost of a babysitter (or two) who can be with the kids in a different part of the house. In this way, parents don't have to be away from their children all evening when their children are too young to be left at home. A second option is to use one home for the kids and a second home (close by or a phone call away) for the adults. A third idea is to rotate the responsibility of providing a lesson or care for the children either in the same home or in another home nearby. This can be an incredible blessing for kids. Finally, the most common idea is to decide that you need to have a night to invest in your spiritual lives individually or as a couple, and to make your own arrangements for child care. No matter what decision the group makes, the best approach is to dialogue openly about both the problem and the solution.

LEADER'S NOTES

Congratulations! You have responded to the call to help shepherd Jesus' flock. There are few other tasks in the family of God that surpass the contribution you will be making.

You can obtain the *Heaven DVD* companion for this discussion guide separately or as part of a *Heaven Leader's Pack* or *Group Kit*. We have cross-referenced the *Heaven* book to the questions in this discussion guide for your reference.

We have provided you several ways to prepare for your role as leader of your small group. Between the *Read Me First*, these *Leader's Notes*, and the Watch This First and Leader Lifter segments on the DVD you'll have all you need to do a great job of leading your group. Just don't forget, you are not alone. God knew that you would be asked to lead this group and he won't let you down. In Hebrews 13:5b *God promises us, Never will I leave you; never will I forsake you...* (NIV).

Your role as leader is to create a safe warm environment for your group. As a leader, your most important job is to create an atmosphere where people are willing to talk honestly about what the topics discussed in this study have to do with them. Be available before people arrive so you can greet them at the door. People are naturally nervous at a new group, so a hug or handshake can help put them at ease.

Prepare for each meeting ahead of time. Before you start leading your group a little preparation will give you confidence. Review the *Read Me First* at the front of your discussion guide so you'll understand the purpose of each section, enabling you to help your group understand it as well. Take the time to review the session, the *Leader's Notes* and Leader Lifter for the session before each session. Also write down your answers to each question. Pay special attention to exercises that ask group members to *do* something. These exercises will help your group live out what the Bible teaches, not just talk about it. Be sure you understand how the exercises work, and bring any supplies you might need, such a paper or pens. Pray for your group members by name at least once between sessions and before each session. Use the *Prayer and Praise Report* each meeting so you will remember prayer requests. Ask God to use your time together to touch the heart of every person. Expect God to give you the opportunity to talk with those he wants you to encourage or challenge in a special way.

Subgrouping. If your group has more than seven people, break into discussion groups of three to four people for the *Growing* and *Prayer and Surrender* sections each week. People will connect more with the study and each other when they have more opportunity to participate. Smaller discussion circles encourage quieter people to talk more and tend to minimize the effects of more vocal or dominant members. Also, people who are unaccustomed to praying aloud will feel more comfortable praying within a smaller group of people. Share prayer requests in the larger group and then break into smaller groups to pray for each other. People are more willing to pray in small circles if they know that the whole group will hear all the prayer requests.

Memorizing Scripture. At the start of each session you will find a memory verse—a verse for the group to memorize each week. Encourage your group members to do this. Memorizing God's Word is both directed and celebrated throughout the Bible, either explicitly (*Your word I have hidden in my heart, that I might not sin against You!* Psalm 119:11), or implicitly, as in the example of our Lord (*...He departed to the mountain to pray.* Mark 6:46).

Anyone who has memorized Scripture can confirm the amazing spiritual benefits that result from this practice. Don't miss out on the opportunity to encourage your group to grow in the knowledge of God's Word through Scripture memorization.

During group meetings. As you begin, have someone in the group read the memory verse and opening paragraphs and then move right into the *Connecting* section. You might want to ask someone in advance of the meeting, because many people are uncomfortable reading aloud in public.

Allow the group an opportunity to discuss their expectations for the study during the first session. Let each person share what he or she hopes to get out of the study. Review the *Group Values* in session one in advance so you can help everyone understand what the group values and goals will be.

In order to maximize your time together and honor the diversity of personality types in your group, do your best to begin and end your sessions on time. You may even want to adjust your starting or stopping time, if necessary. Don't hesitate to open in prayer even before everyone is seated. This isn't disrespectful of those who are still gathering—it respects those who are ready to begin, and the others won't be offended.

If your group is new or if new members have joined you, your top priority is to make them feel welcome. Many people who visit new groups never return because they don't feel like people care or there's a clique that they just can't crash into. So when they walk in, greet them at the door. Give them a hug or a handshake. Look them in the eye when they talk. As your meeting starts, ask everyone to introduce themselves briefly.

Have someone read the Bible passages aloud. It's a good idea to ask someone ahead of time, because not everyone is comfortable reading aloud in public. When the passage has been read, ask the questions that follow. It is not necessary that everyone answer every question. In fact, a group can become boring if you simply go around the circle and give answers. Your goal is to create discussion—which means that perhaps only a few people respond to each question and an engaging dialogue gets going. It's even fine to skip some questions in order to spend more time on questions you believe are most important.

During discussion time, don't forget to give encouragement when people offer answers. Even if someone's answer is difficult to understand, remember that it takes a tremendous step of faith, especially in new groups, to say something early on.

Share prayer requests. It is important to allow time for the group to share prayer requests and praises each week. This is likely the most important part of bonding your group and building deep relational connections. Be sure to encourage the group to keep a record of requests and praises on the *Prayer and Praise Report* pages beginning on page 123. Reviewing ongoing requests and praises encourages the group as they recall God's faithfulness.

Keep your group open. Cast the vision, as Jesus did, to be inclusive not exclusive. The lessons you are learning in your group are things everyone needs to learn. So encourage the group to invite people they know to visit the group each week.

PERSONAL HEALTH PLAN

This worksheet could become your single most important feature in this study. On it you can record your personal priorities before the Father. It will help you live a healthy spiritual life, balancing all five of God's purposes.

PURPOSE	PLAN
CONNECT	WHO are you connecting with spiritually?
GROW	WHAT is your next step for growth?
DEVELOP	WHERE are you serving?
SHARE	WHEN are you shepherding another in Christ?
SURRENDER	HOW are you giving more of your heart to God?

PERSONAL HEALTH ASSESSMENT

	Just Beginning	Getting Going	Well Developed

CONNECTING WITH GOD'S FAMILY

I am deepening my understanding of and
friendship with God in community with others.   1 2 3 4 5

I am growing in my ability both to share and to
show my love to others.   1 2 3 4 5

I am willing to share my real needs for prayer
and support from others.   1 2 3 4 5

I am resolving conflict constructively and am
willing to forgive others.   1 2 3 4 5

CONNECTING Total _____

GROWING TO BE MORE LIKE CHRIST

I have a growing relationship with God through regular
time in the Bible and in prayer (spiritual habits).   1 2 3 4 5

I am experiencing more of the characteristics of
Jesus Christ (love, patience, gentleness, kindness,
self-control, etc.) in my life.   1 2 3 4 5

I am avoiding addictive behaviors (food, television,
busyness, and the like) to meet my needs.   1 2 3 4 5

I am spending time with a Christian friend (spiritual
partner) who celebrates and challenges my spiritual
growth.   1 2 3 4 5

GROWING Total _____

DEVELOPING YOUR GIFTS TO SERVE OTHERS

I have discovered and am further developing my
unique God-given design.   1 2 3 4 5

I am regularly praying for God to show me
opportunities to serve Him and others.   1 2 3 4 5

I am serving in a regular (once a month or more)
ministry in the church or community.   1 2 3 4 5

I am a team player in my small group by sharing
some group role or responsibility.   1 2 3 4 5

DEVELOPING Total _____

SHARING YOUR LIFE MISSION EVERY DAY

I am cultivating relationships with non-Christians
and praying for God to give me natural opportunities
to share his love.   1 2 3 4 5

I am praying and learning about where God can use
me and our group cross-culturally for missions.   1 2 3 4 5

I am investing my time in another person or group
who needs to know Christ.   1 2 3 4 5

I am regularly inviting unchurched or unconnected
friends to my church or small group.   1 2 3 4 5

SHARING Total _____

PRAYER AND SURRENDER

I am experiencing more of the presence and power
of God in my everyday life.   1 2 3 4 5

I am faithfully attending services and my small group
and worshipping God.   1 2 3 4 5

I am seeking to please God by surrendering every area
of my life (health, decisions, finances, relationships,
future, etc.) to Him.   1 2 3 4 5

I am accepting the things I cannot change and becoming
increasingly grateful for the life I've been given.   1 2 3 4 5

PRAYER Total _____

	Connecting	Growing	Serving	Sharing	Surrendering	
20						Well Developed
16						Very Good
12						Getting Going
8						Fair
4						Just Beginning

○ Beginning Assessment Total _____   □ Ending Assessment Total _____

SERVING THE LORD'S SUPPER

...The Lord Jesus, on the night he was betrayed, took bread, and when he had given thanks, he broke it and said, 'This is my body, which is for you; do this in remembrance of me.' In the same way, after supper he took the cup, saying, 'This cup is the new covenant in my blood; do this, whenever you drink, in remembrance of me.' For whenever you eat this bread and drink this cup, you proclaim the Lord's death until he comes.

1 Corinthians 11:23–26

Steps in Serving the Lord's Supper

1. Open by sharing about God's love, forgiveness, grace, mercy, commitment, tenderheartedness, faithfulness, etc., out of your personal journey (connect with the stories of those in the room).

2. Read the passage: *...The Lord Jesus, on the night he was betrayed, took bread, and when he had given thanks, he broke it and said, 'This is my body, which is for you; do this in remembrance of me.'*

3. Pray and pass the bread around the circle (could be time for quiet reflection, singing a simple praise song, or listening to a worship tape).

4. When everyone has been served, remind them that this represents Jesus' broken body on their behalf. Simply state, *Jesus said, 'Do this in remembrance of me.'* Let us eat together, and eat the bread as a group.

5. Then read the rest of the passage: *...In the same way, after supper he took the cup, saying, 'This cup is the new covenant in my blood; do this, whenever you drink it, in remembrance of me.'*

6. Pray and serve the cups, either by passing a small tray, serving them individually, or having members pick up a cup from the table.

7. When everyone has been served, remind them the juice represents Christ's blood shed for them, then simply state, "Take and drink in remembrance of Him. Let us drink together."

8. Finish by singing a simple song, listening to a praise song, or having a time of prayer in thanks to God.

Several Practical Tips in Serving the Lord's Supper

Be sensitive to timing in your meeting.

1. Break up pieces of cracker or soft bread on a small plate or tray. Don't use large servings of bread or grape juice. We recommend using grape juice, not wine, to avoid the possibility of causing a brother to stumble.

2. Prepare all of the elements beforehand and bring these into the room when you are ready.

Communion passages: Matthew 26:26–29; Mark 14:22–25; Luke 22:14–20; 1 Corinthians 10:16–21, 11:17–34

PERFORMING A FOOT-WASHING

Special Note: Foot-washing may not be part of some group member's church tradition and some may be uncomfortable doing this for a variety of reasons. Though we encourage your group to participate, this exercise is optional—it should not become a dividing issue for those troubled by it. It is one idea that is purely optional.

Scripture to Look At: John 13:1–17. In John 13, Jesus makes it quite clear to His disciples that His position as the Father's Son includes being a servant rather than being one of power and glory only. To properly understand the scene and the intention of Jesus, we must realize that the washing of feet was the duty of slaves and indeed of non-Jewish rather than Jewish slaves. Jesus placed Himself in the position of a servant. He displayed to the disciples self-sacrifice and love. (*"...that you also should do what I have done to you."* John 13:15) In view of His majesty, only the symbolic position of a slave was adequate to open their eyes and keep them from lofty illusions. The point of foot-washing, then, is to correct the attitude that Jesus discerned in the disciples. It symbolizes the servant attitude for mutual service, service in your group and for the community around you, which is laid on all Christians.

WHEN TO IMPLEMENT

Knowing when to implement a foot-washing is a sensitive issue. We recommend this foot-washing as one of three options for your surrendering exercise during the last session of your study.

HOW TO PREPARE

What you need:

- ☐ Towels: For the washing and drying of each set of feet.

- ☐ Bowls: Make sure you have enough bowls to be able to have fresh water for washing and rinsing.

- ☐ Liquid Soap: Not a necessity, but a nice touch.

Things to be considerate of:

- ☐ The opposite sex: Men wash men's feet, women wash women's feet.

- ☐ Religious upbringing: Be sensitive to where your group is coming from.

- ☐ Know your group: Be sensitive to the bonding of your group. Make sure you have enough meetings under your belt for your group to know your heart and get the full impact of the foot-washing.

- ☐ Know your options: If someone in your group has limitations (i.e., a lady may come wearing stockings, person may have an open wound or cast) or is uncomfortable with the washing of feet, see if you can wash the hands, see if the spouse (if there is one) can wash the feet, and give the person the right to "pass."

Attitude and objectives:

- ☐ Be in an attitude of prayer for what God can do in and through you. Communicate servanthood. Understand the attitude of humility (both on the "giving" and "receiving" end). Pray for the best time to do a foot-washing in your group. Timing is everything.

Some Additional Ideas:

- ☐ After the foot-washing, you may want to give each member of your group a new pair of socks to put on to enjoy the rest of the group time.

- ☐ Before sending a member of the group on a mission trip or to start a new group, do a foot-washing to serve them before they go out to serve.

SURRENDERING AT THE CROSS

Surrendering everything to God is one of the most challenging aspects of following Jesus. It involves a relationship, one which is built on trust and faith. Each of us is in a different place on our spiritual journey. Some of us have known the Lord for many years, some are new in our faith, and some may still be checking God out. Regardless, we all have things that we still want control over—things we don't want to give to God because we don't know what He will do with them. These things are truly more important to us than God is—they have become our god.

We need to understand that God wants us to be completely devoted to Him. Luke 10:27 says, *"Love the Lord your God with all your heart and with all your soul and with all your strength and with all your mind...."* If we truly love God with all our heart, soul, strength, and mind, we will be willing to give Him everything.

Steps in Surrendering at the Cross:

1. You will need some small pieces of paper and pens or pencils for people to write down the things they want to sacrifice/surrender to God.

2. If you have a wooden cross, hammers, and nails you can have the members nail their sacrifices to the cross. If you don't have a wooden cross—get creative. Think of another way to symbolically relinquish the sacrifices to God. Consider making a styrofoam or cardboard cross and use push-pins to nail the sacrifices to the cross. Or you might use a fireplace, fire pit, or barbeque to burn them in the fire as an offering to the Lord. The point is giving to the Lord whatever hinders your relationship with Him.

3. Create an atmosphere conducive to quiet reflection and prayer. Consider softly playing music that draws you quietly to God with hearts focused on hearing from Him. Whatever this quiet atmosphere looks like for your group, do the best you can to create a peaceful time to meet with God.

4. Once you are settled, prayerfully think about the points below. Let the words and thoughts draw you into a heart-to-heart connection with your Lord Jesus Christ.

    - Worship Him. Ask God to change your viewpoint so you can worship Him through a surrendered spirit.

    - Humble yourself. Surrender doesn't happen without humility. James 4:6–7 says, *"...'God opposes the proud but gives grace to the humble.' Submit yourselves, then, to God...."*

    - Surrender your mind, will, and emotions. This is often the toughest part of surrendering. Romans 6:13 says, *"Do not offer the parts of your body to sin, as instruments of wickedness, but rather offer yourselves to God, as those who have been brought from death to life; and offer the parts of your body to him as instruments of righteousness."* What do you sense God urging you to give to Him so you can have the kind of intimacy He desires with you? Our hearts yearn for this kind of connection with Him; let go of the things that stand between you.

    - Write out your prayer: Write out your prayer of sacrifice and surrender to the Lord. This may be an attitude, a fear, a person, a job, a possession—anything that God reveals is a hindrance to your relationship with Him.

5. Nail your sacrifice to the Cross, or burn it as a sacrifice in the fire: After writing out your sacrifice, symbolically take it to the cross and offer it to the Lord.

6. Close by singing, praying together, or taking Communion: Make this time as short or as long as seems appropriate for your group.

Surrendering to God is life-changing and liberating. God desires that we be over-comers! 1 John 4:4 says, *"You, dear children, are from God and have overcome...because the one who is in you is greater than the one who is in the world."*

SMALL GROUP ROSTER

Name	Address	Phone	Email Address	Team or Role	Church Ministry
Bill Jones	7 Alvalar Street L.F. 92665	766-2255	bjones@aol.com	Socials	Children's Ministry

(Pass your book around your group at your first meeting to get everyone's name and contact information.)

Name	Address	Phone	Email Address	Team or Role	Church Ministry

SMALL GROUP CALENDAR

Planning ahead with a calendar can help ensure the greatest participation at every meeting. At the end of each meeting, review this calendar. Be sure to include a regular rotation of host homes and leaders, and don't forget birthdays, socials, church events, holidays, and mission/ministry projects.

Date	Session	Host Home	Dessert/Meal	Leader
Monday, Dec. 4	1	Steve and Laura's	Joe	Bill

PRAYER AND PRAISE REPORT

Share prayer requests in the large group and then break into smaller groups of two to four for prayer. Smaller groups give everyone the opportunity to share and be prayed for.

Date: Prayer Request/Praise Report

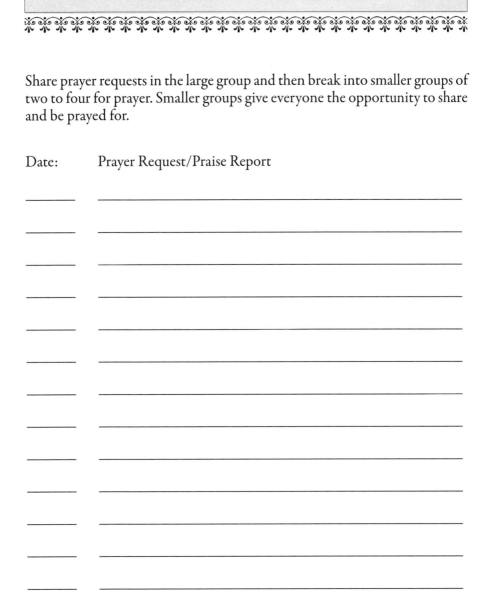

PRAYER AND PRAISE REPORT

Share prayer requests in the large group and then break into smaller groups of two to four for prayer. Smaller groups give everyone the opportunity to share and be prayed for.

Date: Prayer Request/Praise Report

_____ _____

_____ _____

_____ _____

_____ _____

_____ _____

_____ _____

_____ _____

_____ _____

_____ _____

_____ _____

_____ _____

_____ _____

_____ _____

PRAYER AND PRAISE REPORT

Share prayer requests in the large group and then break into smaller groups of two to four for prayer. Smaller groups give everyone the opportunity to share and be prayed for.

Date: Prayer Request/Praise Report

_____   _____

_____   _____

_____   _____

_____   _____

_____   _____

_____   _____

_____   _____

_____   _____

_____   _____

_____   _____

_____   _____

_____   _____

_____   _____

PRAYER AND PRAISE REPORT

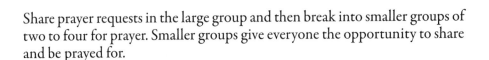

Share prayer requests in the large group and then break into smaller groups of two to four for prayer. Smaller groups give everyone the opportunity to share and be prayed for.

Date: Prayer Request/Praise Report

_____   _____

_____   _____

_____   _____

_____   _____

_____   _____

_____   _____

_____   _____

_____   _____

_____   _____

_____   _____

_____   _____

_____   _____

_____   _____

DEEPENING LIFE TOGETHER SERIES

Deepening Life Together is a series of Bible studies developed to help you grow in a deeper relationship with God and others. The series offers small groups an opportunity to explore biblical subjects in several categories: books of the Bible (Acts, Romans, John Ephesians, Revelation), theology (Promises of God, Parables), and spiritual disciplines (Prayers of Jesus).

Studies in this series include:

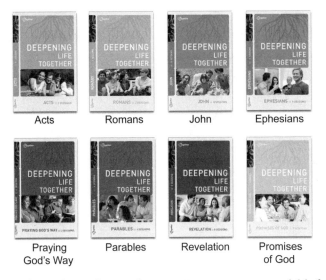

Acts	Romans	John	Ephesians
Praying God's Way	Parables	Revelation	Promises of God

A *Deepening Life Together* Video Teaching DVD companion is available for each study in the series. For each study session, the DVD contains a lesson taught by a master teacher backed by scholars giving their perspective on the subject.

Every study includes activities based on five biblical purposes of the church: Connecting, Growing, Developing, Sharing, and Surrendering. These studies will help your group deepen your walk with God while you discover what he has created you for and how you can turn his desires into an everyday reality in your lives. Experience the transformation firsthand as you begin your deepening your life together for him.

To find out more please go to www.GroupSpice.com or call 619.733.9218.

TERRY CLARK

The *Heaven DVD* companion to this discussion guide contains worship songs by Terry Clark. Terry Clark's voice has been a regular part of Maranatha! Music's productions since the 70's, including 7 years of Promise Keepers.

"More than ever the Body of Christ is recognizing its need to deeply know God. If we ignore the inner cry for intimate communication with God, we become hard of hearing, unable to recognize his voice when he speaks to us."

Terry's music is designed to direct the listener to an intimate relationship with their Heavenly Father.

Terry and his wife, Nancy, continue to produce music projects and live worship and teaching events focused on the core of Christianity—an intimate relationship with God. All their music and materials can be found at CATALYSTPEOPLE.com.

CATALYST MINISTRIES

P.O. BOX 776

San Clemente, CA 92674

Ph: (949) 366-2121

Fax: (949) 366-2104